LEADING THE FOLLOWERS
BY FOLLOWING THE LEADER

A Radical Look at Radical Leadership

LEADING
the
FOLLOWERS
by
FOLLOWING
the
LEADER

DENNIS L. GORTON
with Tom Allen

Christian Publications
3825 Hartzdale Drive, Camp Hill, PA 17011
www.cpi-horizon.com
www.christianpublications.com

Faithful, biblical publishing since 1883

Leading the Followers by Following the Leader
ISBN: 0-87509-892-4
LOC Catalog Card Number: 00-090168
© 2000 by Christian Publications, Inc.
All rights reserved
Printed in the United States of America

00 01 02 03 04   5 4 3 2 1

Contents

Foreword vii

Introduction
A Church in Search of Leadership 1

Chapter 1
The Wealth of a Poor Spirit 13

Chapter 2
Joy in the Mourning 29

Chapter 3
The Strength of Submission....................................43

Chapter 4
In Dependence..63

Chapter 5
Merciful Heavens! 91

Chapter 6
Wholly Holy..113

Chapter 7
The Peacemakers 129

Chapter 8
Testing One, Two, Three 149

Chapter 9
Oh, to Be Like Him! 169

Epilogue
New Hope for the Church....................185

Endnotes 191

Study Guide
Leading the Followers
    by Following the Leader 199

Selected Bibliography........................237

FOREWORD

*T*he Scriptures are clear: We are to "Be fruitful, and multiply" (Genesis 1:28, KJV). But in the same passage, God tells us we can only multiply "according to [our] kind" (1:24). We can only reproduce what we are.

In this book, Dennis Gorton goes to the heart of the issue: Leadership multiplication begins and ends with character. We reproduce who we are.

Jesus' ordination sermon for the twelve apprentice leaders in Matthew 5-7 begins by addressing the heart of the leader. Jesus knew that you can only reproduce who you are, and who you are begins not with our external leadership skills but our internal heart response to the Leader of leaders.

We are commanded in the Scriptures to "make disciples of all nations" (Matthew 28:19). As we pour our energies into "walk[ing] as Jesus did" (1 John 2:6), we will soon realize that the work of ministry begins by keeping our heart in tune with the heart of the Savior. In ministry we quickly look in the mirror and understand that our greatest problem is our own selfish lifestyle.

This book goes to the heart of the matter and helps us see that the primary issue is a matter of the heart.

As I read and reread this book, my heart was warmed, encouraged and challenged again to do ministry "Jesus-style"—reflecting both the character and priorities of Christ.

As *you* read this book, I encourage you to do so with an open Bible, an open heart and a desire to allow the Spirit of God to "guide you into all truth" (John 16:13). Read this with your church leadership team and allow God to work in your midst as together you return to the profound basics of true character-based leadership.

I highly commend this book to you and your leadership team!

Dr. Dann Spader
Executive Director,
SonLife Ministries

A Church in Search of Leadership

*L*eadership—the word itself conjures up a great variety of images. Definitions abound and books on the subject are plentiful. Yet the church struggles with the issue of leadership as well as with leaders. The great plethora of leadership books seems to focus on the skills of leaders and often confuse leadership principles with management and administrative tasks.

A corporate model for church leadership skill development, rather than a discipleship model for leadership multiplication, seems to abound. The corporate model focuses primarily on skill development and an approach that says, "Successful leaders do this. . . . If you do this you too will be successful." The discipleship model is inclusive of both skill development and character development. The two are intertwined. By leadership multiplication I mean a model where leaders are growing into Christlike character while using their skills in church leadership and multiplying their lives in emerging leaders who will grow the same character for leadership. It is the Second Timothy 2:2 model as seen in the life of Christ as He developed leaders for a movement of multiplying churches.

The corporate and discipleship leadership models are distinctly different—the outcomes not even in the same ballpark. The discipleship model seeks an outcome of life transformation while the corporate model tends to focus on task accomplishment. While the two models can learn from each other, especially in the context of today's culture, let me be clear that what the church needs is a discipleship model of leadership multiplication that focuses on character and relationship if we are going to be a culturally relevant church that is winning its community to Christ, building them up into Christ, and equipping them to serve Christ both in the church and in His harvest.

A Lack of Relevance

In 1990, George Barna conducted an extensive survey among unchurched people. One of his questions was simple but loaded: "Is the church today relevant?" The response was quite foreboding: Almost two-thirds of those who answered the question said no.[1] To add insult to injury, Barna also reports, "Only a small proportion of adults say they would turn to the church for help in a time of personal crisis."[2]

What an incredible indictment! There was a time when the church was esteemed as a prominent if not dominant force in our culture. People searching for hope and meaning knew where to turn. But by staying away in droves, vast numbers of Americans are confirming our worst nightmare: The church seems irrelevant. We are not meeting even the very basic needs which Christ called us to fulfill. We have comforted ourselves with some church growth, but statistics indicate we have been shuffling the saints between churches, not building the kingdom through conversion growth.

The description of the 200 leaders from the tribe of Issachar—"men . . . who understood the times and knew what Israel should do" (1 Chronicles 12:32)—does not apply to many of our churches today.

A Lack of Confidence

Barna's research further indicates that "Confidence in the Church as a social institution is declining steadily. For many years, the Church stood as the most revered social institution. Today, it ranks third or fourth on the list."[3]

The Princeton Religious Research Center tracked the changes in confidence in selected American institutions from 1979 to 1987. While trust in the Supreme Court and the military increased during those years (by 7 percent and 6 percent respectively), confidence in church and organized religion *declined* 4 percent. It should be noted that this survey was completed *before* the widely publicized moral failures of televangelists Jim Bakker (1987) and Jimmy Swaggart (1988). More recent studies indicate those statistics are still going south.

George Barna interprets these ominous numbers for us:

> A growing percentage of adults believe that the Church at large is losing its influence upon society. This is important because we know that Americans—especially

Boomers—do not want to associate with a "loser," whether it is a person or an organization.[4]

A Lack of Growth

As we look at the evangelical landscape of large churches—both "super" and "mega" congregations—one might assume that the church overall is healthy and growing in the United States. But research indicates that what is really happening might be called "the reshuffling of the saints." The actual community of believers is not expanding in any dramatic way. Rather it is being consolidated in huge churches that are attracting believers from declining congregations. An estimated 90 million adults in America have been "church shopping."[5] The Barna Research Group makes this comment on the megachurch trend:

> This is growth by transfer, rather than by conversion. . . . [W]hile many churches across the nation receive attention for their explosive growth, relatively few of those churches are attracting adults who are newcomers to the faith. Most frequently, they are enlisting individuals who have left their existing church home to be part of the "happening" church.[6]

The bottom line is this: Most churches in America today have fewer than 100 people in attendance on any single day of worship. According to 1998 statistics from my own denomination, The Christian and

Missionary Alliance, 66.9 percent of our congregations have 100 or less in Sunday morning attendance. If the average attendance number is increased to 200 or less, the percentage rises to 87.7 percent.[7] These churches are small but of most concern is not their smallness but the fact that they stay small year after year because of a lack of conversion growth.

It is also discouraging to note that nearly two-thirds of the churches in The Christian and Missionary Alliance (C&MA) are classified as "non- growing."[8] Conversion growth statistics paint an even more grim picture when we realize that in 1997, 48 percent of all churches reported zero conversions for the year. This would not be so utterly disconcerting except for the fact that the C&MA overall has recorded some of the *better* numbers when it comes to church growth!

Can everything be reduced to numbers? Should it be? Is God's blessing on a church or denomination evidenced only in its numerical growth (or lack thereof)? This would certainly be an oversimplification. But we are still left with some difficult questions to ponder:

- How can we claim to live and communicate an exciting, life-changing message while we watch our congregations decline in membership and enthusiasm?
- How can we associate ourselves with the anointed, influential, and outreach-focused early church in the book of Acts with its explosive, sustained growth?
- How is it possible that thousands of evangelical churches can operate for a full year with-

out a single convert to show for all their
time, money and effort?

This is more than troubling—it's *tragic*!

So, what's wrong with this picture?

A Lack of Leadership

As early as 1934, Ordway Tead said, "On every
hand today the cry is for more and better leaders."[9]
In 1976, LeRoy Eims insisted, "A crisis of leadership engulfs the world. Political leaders, economic
experts, editorial writers, newsmen, spokesmen in
the fields of education and religion raise the hue
and cry: Men who know the way and can lead others on the right path are few."[10] Peter Wagner offered this insight in 1984: "[I]f churches are going
to maximize their growth potential, they need pastors who are strong leaders."[11]

The consensus has been building: The quality of
leadership has a direct impact on the success or failure of a church. That is why, in the 1980s, religious
writers waxed eloquent on this subject, though few
bothered to develop a meaningful theological perspective. Management and guidance were carefully
scrutinized from an observational perspective; however, very little was established from a biblical, philo-
sophical perspective. It was about leadership skill and
style more than substance.

Christ: Character-Driven Style

Jesus Christ, however, has a totally different approach. He moves from character to skill development and style. His perspective is that leadership

begins and ends with character. Leadership skills, though vital and important, may help the church be the church, but apart from godly character that drives and impacts those skills and styles, the fix will be temporary. A critical issue in the church today is that we have often failed to recognize character transformation as a prerequisite for leadership. We need to consider that only out of a transformed temperament can grow a godly leadership manner that will get things done while transforming lives in the process. But the end never justifies the means. If we run roughshod over people while trying to build His kingdom, we do more harm than good.

Christ's kind of leadership ensures that the church will always have qualified leaders. Christlike leaders seek out others so qualified to mentor them into leadership as well—and not just for the purpose of having enough help. It is to provide the *right kind* of leaders to give direction to the body of Christ.

Our Savior illustrated this in the development of His followers. By far the largest concentration of His time during three years of intense ministry was given to the building, equipping and leadership development of twelve men. This was time well spent as evidenced in the remarkable events recorded in the book of Acts.

But it began with observation of the Leader's life and became clearly focused in His leadership workshop. Christ taught them principles for the effectual leading of His Church. Recorded in Matthew 5-7, it is known as "The Sermon on the Mount."

It was at this time that Jesus took His apprentice leaders aside (even though others listened in) and began to instruct them on issues that would greatly impact the Church. As one studies the Gospels, it becomes clear that this teaching marks a turning point in Jesus' ministry: He begins to focus more and more on training the Twelve to lead the Church of the future. It turns out that this "sermon" is the most important workshop on leadership ever given.

It is interesting to observe the ministry years of the life of Christ and to discover that He began His ministry by calling people from among the religious lost (people who knew about God but did not know Him personally) to become His followers. He spent significant time building them into knowledgeable followers whose lives were being changed by Christ's own values. He walked them through overlapping phases of ministry by focusing their lives on the harvest and equipping them to become workers in that harvest. When they were sufficiently trained as workers He more clearly identified those of His followers who had leadership skills and began to develop them as leaders. This phase of His ministry began with the instruction on leadership character we see in Matthew 5-7.

In more recent years, church management and growth literature has done an admirable job of teaching how to enlarge and manage a congregation. But little has been said about leadership—about who they should be and how church leaders should care for themselves so that they can be effective in directing the flock of God. Leadership focuses on modeling and empowering the vision while management seeks to administer the mission. With management taking the forefront in our time, vision casting is often overlooked. The discipleship model of leadership requires both modeling and empowering vision and managing mission. Christlike leaders must set the example in both being like Him and empowering and managing the work of His Church. This is the thrust of Christ's teaching in Matthew 5-7. The Lord Jesus trained His followers in those principles that would cause them to live a quality of life which others would want to emulate.

So it is that Jesus makes this radical claim: We can only lead the followers by following the Leader. Revolutionary? Contradictory? Read on. I firmly believe that the reason for little conversion growth in churches and denominations can be traced to a misunderstanding of kingdom leadership principles. We have failed to produce and multiply Christlike leaders who have modeled their ministry after the Master.

Join me now in a journey to the very heart of the kind of followership and leadership which is patterned after the Lord Jesus Christ—a ministry of multiplying leaders whose drive is to be Christlike in life and leadership as they use their God-given skills and abilities for His kingdom.

LEADERSHIP REFLECTIONS

1. Consider the importance of leadership to the future of the Church. Is Christlikeness really an option?
2. Study a harmony of the Gospels: Do you see a new phase of ministry focusing on leadership beginning with Matthew 5-7? Discuss the implications of applying these principles to all followers, but especially to leaders.

HUMILITY

IN COMING FACE TO face with God, a leader sees the poverty of his spirit as it relates to the Lord's holiness. He admits, "I need You, Lord," and thus begins his journey to holiness.

CHAPTER ONE

The Wealth of a Poor Spirit

> *Blessed are the poor in spirit,*
> *for theirs is the kingdom of heaven.*
> *(Matthew 5:3)*

In his book, *Joy Comes in the Mourning*, David Johnson comments on the intriguing background of the sermon given in Matthew 5. Jesus had performed many miracles: the lame walked; the blind were given sight; demons were cast out. Massive crowds began to form and the disciples were beginning to feel that they had made a wise choice. They excitedly anticipated the power, glory and status that their association with the Messiah would bring them.

But at the height of it all, this man named Jesus did something inexplicable. Instead of working the crowd or trying to figure out how to maintain the crowd, even how to increase the crowd—He withdrew from the crowd. "Now when he saw the crowds, he went up on a mountainside and sat down" (Matthew 5:1).

13

This was a very curious, seemingly ill-timed move on Christ's part. Can't you just hear what the disciples might have wanted to say to Him: "What are You doing withdrawing from these adoring masses? You've got a major movement going! You have just become the pastor of 'The First Church of What's Happening Now.' . . ."[1]

Johnson goes on to suggest that today's church growth consultants would recommend against the timing of Christ's withdrawal. It looks like a bad idea—erratic behavior that could derail a movement, just when it seemed to be gaining that all-important momentum. One is tempted to ask what Jesus' agenda could possibly be. If not crowds and momentum, then what? Could it be that a movement of those who would truly become Christlike followers was more important than superficial crowds?

Christ's withdrawal also contradicted the disciples' expectations about the Messiah. The Christ was supposed to come and establish a Jewish kingdom; these twelve men expected to play a strategic part in overthrowing the Roman government.

Little did they know that for Jesus and them this was a transition moment—a new phase of His ministry in which He would emphasize leadership development. While the teaching in Matthew 5-7 is truly foundational for all believers, Jesus focused the sermon on His apprentice leaders. Soon His twelve leaders would take up new responsibility. They needed to be ready and Jesus was determined to get them off to a good start.

No doubt the disciples were wondering what their Master was about to tell them. It had to be something earth-shaking and life-transforming— what else could be so urgent that it justified pulling the plug on everything that was happening? But when they finally heard what He had to say, the Twelve must have been stunned by its unexpectedness.

Leadership 101: Humility

With boldness and persuasion, Jesus Christ began His workshop on leadership with the principle of *humility*. Unbelievable as it may seem, this was the first foundational truth our Lord wanted to convey to those who would shepherd His flock in the months and years to come: *God blesses and works through those who realize their need for Him.* Jesus knew that humility would grow in these apprentice leaders only as they were immersed in the knowledge and experience of the Father. He knew that they would not merely *become* humble, but that they needed to *practice* humility in order to truly lead His church.

I truly love Gary Thomas' words that apply this truth for leaders and followers today:

> In all of our discipleship, we teach prayer, we teach Bible study, and we teach evangelism. These are necessary disciplines. But without the interior foundation of humility, they can't possibly support our spiritual house. To experience the life of Christ, we

> need the inner discipline of humility. . . .
> [T]he solution isn't to neglect the outer dis-
> ciplines, it's to begin practicing the inner
> disciplines as well, beginning with Christ's
> foundational attitude of humility.[2]

Whatever happened to the *coup d'état* of Rome's
political leaders? This didn't sound one bit like the
power encounter they had been expecting from their
Messiah! In fact, they might have paused, as we
must, and thought about that word "blessed" that Jesus used as well. How does this affect leaders and
their leadership?

The word "blessed" literally means "happy." Christ
emphasizes through repetition that the truly fulfilled
person is the one who derives his inner joy from God.
His contentment is not based on possessions or favorable circumstances. Such blessedness is an internal characteristic produced by the Holy Spirit in the
life of every person who commits to becoming like
Christ in these character qualities. While applicable
to everyone (such as the crowds who listened in on
Jesus' instruction), these character traits are essential
for leaders in His church. The first of these traits is
humility.

Our society's view on this is quite different. The
secular world wants us to believe that our happiness
depends on our level of personal achievement and
material wealth. To be blessed, we must put our best
foot forward and arrogantly sell ourselves. In the
words of Allan Bloom, "We are selves, and everything we do is to satisfy our selves. . . . Be yourself."[3]

The Savior offers a radically distinct perspective. We will be blessed to the extent that we understand the full impact of being "poor in spirit."

So just what does it mean? David Johnson offers these insights:

> Defined bluntly, *poor in spirit* means, "with reference to the spirit, a poverty." The Greek word is *ptochos*, and its expanded nuance includes "one who is reduced to begging dependence; one who is broken." The Contemporary English Version of Matthew 5:3 captures the essence: "God blesses those people who depend only on him."[4]

The New Living Translation also reflects the meaning of the Greek; it says that God blesses those who "realize their need for him."

When we think of Christ Jesus, we generally think of Him as a very capable person, but His own self-testimony was that "the Son can do nothing by himself," according to John 5:19. It was not that Jesus was helpless, but that He chose dependency on the Father because His driving desire was to think, behave and do what the Father was doing. His leadership was the Father's leadership. In John 7:16 He reiterated His dependency when He declared that even His teaching was not His but was from the Father. If Jesus Himself practiced total dependency on the Father for His ministry, it seems only logical that we too must develop the discipline of character that leads to dependency. That discipline is humility and humility is born in our beings as we are overwhelmed in our experience with God by who He is and who we are.

Jesus desires us to know about the great wealth of a poor spirit, one that is totally dependent on God. There is something very deep and profound about recognizing our own inability while being awed with His total sufficiency. This quality of character is not optional for a pastor and his leaders. Rather, it is an all-essential first.

Humility and Leadership

Christ illustrated the importance of humility as a leadership characteristic by pointing to a very familiar group of leaders who had set a negative example: "For I tell you that unless your righteousness surpasses that of the Pharisees and the teachers of the law, you will certainly not enter the kingdom of heaven" (Matthew 5:20).

This must have been confusing to the disciples. From childhood they had been taught that the Pharisees and teachers of religious law were to be revered as holy men of God. The people were expected to listen to what these leaders said and follow their example. What could Jesus possibly mean by openly condemning their righteousness as inadequate?

The Pharisees and religious teachers were totally inadequate for leadership in God's kingdom because, despite their apparent obedience, they lacked a godly character. They utterly rejected the way of humility and in its place they substituted self-righteousness. Such pseudo-leaders had not experienced genuine internal change. They had the leadership skills, but not the character.

The Savior's warning in Matthew 5:20 also reminded His followers that God's standard for righteousness is literally impossible to attain without Christ's invasion into the human heart. Even those who appeared to be veritable paragons of virtue fell far short of the new covenant standard that the Messiah insisted upon.

The Pharisees, chief priests and religious teachers had style without substance. Lacking the character quality of humility, they did more damage than good. This is why Christ lambasted these blind leaders who had misled so many into a legalistic nightmare. All of the emphasis in the world on obeying rules will not produce godly character. But the humble leader who is utterly dependent on God will have the desire and power to live a righteous lifestyle and lead a movement.

To be "poor in spirit" means to humbly recognize our utter dependence upon the Lord. Without His righteousness, we have none at all. The religious leaders of Jesus' day could not accept this. They were determined to crank out their own version of moral and ethical behavior. Those efforts amounted to filthy rags in God's sight.

Christlike leadership begins with the somber recognition of our fallen condition. We must truly believe that Paul's declaration, "For all have sinned and fall short of the glory of God" (Romans 3:23), applies to us as well. It is impossible for us to achieve the lofty criterion of righteousness which would make us acceptable to our Creator. Coming face to face with the Holy One, we must confess our poverty of spirit. If we are ever to be holy as He is holy, we will need Him to accomplish that in our lives.

Many in our churches today would call themselves believers. They attend the services and think that they know God, but they have never understood the wealth of a poor spirit. These people would do anything to avoid being humbled before the Lord or anyone else. By avoiding this great truth of kingdom living, however, they have limited their capacity for truly knowing the Lord. Unfortunately, many of these same people are elected to leadership positions within the fellowship. And they are in no way ready to lead others because they do not want to be "poor in spirit." They are often more concerned with power and control, position and influence. They focus on what they think is good for the church rather than learning what God is doing and getting into the middle of it.

Some of them may be pastors or members of the governing board. Outwardly, they appear to have the skills for leadership. They may be intelligent, diligent and sincere. But the pride of their hearts eventually betrays them. They become a destructive force by inciting petty disputes and flagrantly rejecting the needs and concerns of others. Their attitude is, "It's my way or the highway!"

Leadership must begin with a genuine desire for humility. A godly leader will grow and develop only to the extent that he or she keeps coming back to this principle. Becoming "poor in spirit" is a process which the Lord Jesus keeps working in us so that we can know Him more intimately and lead more effectively. Repeatedly, we need to be brought to the place where we recognize some area of sin that needs to be cleansed.

James reminds us that if we humble ourselves before the Lord, He will lift us up (4:10). In this way, the humble leader dwells on a higher spiritual plane and is continually being refreshed by God. He is being made to see *what he is* and *what he can become* as the direct result of God's work on the inside.

Humility and Holiness

In *The Knowledge of the Holy*, A. W. Tozer says,

> Until we have seen ourselves as God sees us, we are not likely to be disturbed over conditions around us as long as they do not get so far out of hand as to threaten our comfortable way of life. We have learned to live with unholiness.[5]

Away from the glaring light of our Creator's utter holiness, we can begin to think that we are spiritually OK. But once exposed to His ultimate purity, our own moral repugnance becomes readily apparent. This is a humbling experience as described by Isaiah:

> In the year that King Uzziah died, I saw the Lord seated on a throne, high and exalted, and the train of his robe filled the temple. Above him were seraphs, each with

six wings: With two wings they covered
their faces, with two they covered their feet,
and with two they were flying. And they
were calling to one another:

> "Holy, holy, holy is the LORD Almighty;
>   the whole earth is full of his glory. . . ."

"Woe to me!" I cried. "I am ruined! For I
am a man of unclean lips, and I live among a
people of unclean lips, and my eyes have
seen the King, the LORD Almighty." (Isaiah
6:1-3, 5)

These are the words of a man who had become
"poor in spirit." This was the prophet's graduate
school. The course called Humility 101 prepared him
for both personal holiness and powerful leadership.

Look at God's loving response to this lowly recognition:

> For this is what the high and lofty One
>   says—
> he who lives forever, whose name is holy:
> "I live in a high and holy place,
>   but also with him who is contrite and
>   lowly in spirit,
>   to revive the spirit of the lowly and to
>   revive the heart of the contrite."
> (Isaiah 57:15)

Pastors and church leaders need to come back to
basics. Our pursuit of a holy life begins with the bold
recognition of our complete unholiness. But by doing
this, we are guaranteed the presence and guidance of

God. He chooses to dwell with the humble and contrite rather than those who pretend to have it all together! Leadership is not about who is the most
qualified. Instead, the Lord wants to use those who
understand that they are the least qualified.

Humility and Ability

Humility does not imply a *lack* of confidence or
ability. But the relationship of our skills and abilities
to our character is of great import. The servant leader
who is "poor in spirit" can be brimming with confidence in his ability. Why? Because it is not based on
his own strengths or righteousness—his faith arises
from the character and abilities of Christ within.

Such an attitude is a far cry from the current emphasis on developing one's "self-concept"—but is
understanding ourselves really as important as we
have been led to believe? The Scripture emphasizes
the importance of understanding God as a way to
understand ourselves. When we see that the Creator was willing to send His only Son to die for us,
we begin to see just how much we are valued and
loved. Any appropriate sense of self-image, especially as it relates to the confidence and ability to
lead the church, must be derived from what took
place on the cross.

Once we grasp the great love wherewith we have
been loved, there is no need to focus on ourselves.
This is why Jesus clearly stated that we must not be
self-centered, but concerned more with Him and others: "If anyone would come after me, he must deny
himself and take up his cross daily and follow me. For

whoever wants to save his life will lose it, but whoever loses his life for me will save it" (Luke 9:23-24).

Instead of fighting for our rights, we can relate to one another based on our experience with God. Our view of others will be right because we see ourselves as being poor in spirit. The common bond that puts all of us on an equal plane is our hopelessness apart from the Lord. This realization gives us grace and mercy in our hearts for other sinners. This is why David Schroeder says that the Beatitudes can be reduced to one word—*humility*—which he describes as "a disposition toward life that holds values and priorities that are far higher and more worthy than the individual 'rights' for which so many people constantly seem to be fighting."[6]

Humility and Relationships

Leadership is primarily about relationships. The biblical perspective is this: Relationships with people must be based on our relationship with God—and the foundation of that relationship must be the character quality of *humility*. We approach the Lord in humble recognition of our need for His love and righteousness. And we can best relate to one another when we realize that all of us are together on this pilgrimage in the pursuit of becoming more Christlike. We can bless and help each other as one beggar showing another beggar where he found bread.

This dynamic has tremendous implications as we fulfill various leadership roles. Many people find themselves threatened when they work with others because of feelings of insecurity or inferiority. They are then tempted to withdraw from the group. But we must help them see themselves through God's eyes—loved, wanted and appreciated, with something unique to contribute to the process.

For example, if a pastor finds out that a certain elder never speaks up in a meeting, he should make a conscious effort to get him to talk. "So, Bill, what are your thoughts about our situation here?" This lets Bill know that he and his comments are valued. Bill needs to contribute so that he can share in the ministry of shepherding the flock of God. And it may be that quiet, unassuming leader that has the most substantive things to say.

Another instance where humility becomes foundational to our relationships is when a leader needs to humbly admit that he was wrong. The pastor should be an example to others in this area. If the board members know that their shepherd recognizes his own mistakes and is willing to confess them, it will create a healthy atmosphere for everyone else. But if the pastor must always be right, it will send cold shivers of contention among his team members.

———

"Shocking" is a weak word to describe the first phrase that fell from the Savior's lips in Matthew 5. The disciples were ready to hear a "rock 'em, sock 'em" sermon on how to keep this movement growing right up until the overthrow of the Roman government! Instead, they heard, "God blesses those who realize their need for Him."

Of all the things Christ could have said at this pivotal moment in His new movement, this hardly seemed to be what was needed. It was not until after His death and resurrection that the disciples fully appreciated the undeniable importance of the Beatitudes.

So, do you want to be a leader?

Become poor in spirit!

Do you want others to look up to you?

Humble yourself!

Do you want others to follow you?

Lead them in humility!

It's not about "who has the power and authority." Effective leadership emanates from those who humbly recognize that apart from Jesus Christ they are nothing at all and have nothing whatsoever to offer. This is the wealth of a poor spirit.

The next principle packed as much punch as the first.

LEADERSHIP REFLECTIONS:

1. What are the implications of leading the church from a position of humility? How would it change the way you do business as a church?
2. In Luke 9:23-24 what does it mean to "deny himself"? What are the issues this raises in church leadership?

BROKENNESS

A LEADER REALIZES HIS need to mourn his own sin. This repentance produces a contrite heart, which enables him to deal with anger inside and manage interpersonal relationships and conflicts outside.

CHAPTER
TWO

Joy in the Mourning

Blessed are those who mourn,
for they will be comforted.
                              (Matthew 5:4)

he story is told of a minister who brought his little boy to the memorial at Pearl Harbor. They
were looking over the names on a plaque. A bit
confused, the boy asked, "Who are all these people?"
The father replied, "These are the brave soldiers who
died in the service." The boy thought for a moment,
and then inquired, "The *morning* service or the *evening*
service?"

This is an old joke for those who grew up in the
church. But it does have contemporary significance.
"Blessed are those who mourn" might seem like an
invitation to have a sour disposition and a call to lead
a miserable, grumpy life. Some people get on a guilt
trip after reading Matthew 5:4. They are convicted
about being too happy or goofing around too much.

But is that what this text really means? The word
for "mourn" here in the original language is *penthos*.[1]
It is the very strongest of all the words used for
"mourn" in the Greek language. It speaks to the kind
of grief that possesses a person so totally that nothing

else matters at that time. Many who have lost a loved one can relate to this description. One's whole being is obsessed with mourning.

We should understand that "mourning" follows naturally after being "poor in spirit." When we have confronted our moral and spiritual bankruptcy, the obvious result is a sense of brokenness. This contrition is the work of the Holy Spirit in us that produces grieving and repentance for sin. "Repent" can be used in conjunction with "mourn," but one cannot replace the other. True repentance leads to brokenness. Genuine brokenness leads to repentance.

Mourning for our sinfulness is the action of life that results in a broken spirit before God. It is a part of the process that leads us to a lifestyle of discovering our sin and constantly repenting in order to be in right relationship with the Father on whom we depend. The result of this kind of sorrow for sin will ultimately be a contrite character. In this way, the Lord will have us right where He wants us. Remember, God dwells with those who have a humble and contrite heart (Isaiah 57:15).

Repentance and Mourning

The concept of repentance is often misunderstood. In Jesus' time, John the Baptist was one of the foremost speakers along these lines. Here's his take on it: "In those days John the Baptist came, preaching in the Desert of Judea and saying, 'Repent, for the kingdom of heaven is near' " (Matthew 3:1-2).

John is asking his listeners to have a change of mind which leads to a change of action. "Repent"

means to turn completely around. Those heading
due south were commanded to turn 180 degrees
and go north. They were to change their minds
about the kingdom of God. This would result in re-
gret for past misconceptions about that kingdom,
and a willingness to embrace new concepts and behaviors.

This was a vital admonition for this audience. The
Jewish crowd had several misconceptions about the
identity and nature of the Messiah. They were wait-
ing for an earthly king with political clout. Their
Messiah would topple the Roman government and
establish His kingdom with Jewish leadership. Everyone would live happily ever after.

Why did they believe this? Because these were the
teachings of the scribes and Pharisees. The Jews believed that their status as God's chosen people would
give them a special place in the Messiah's new world
order. As physical descendants of Abraham, they believed that they were sinless and accepted before God
unless they committed some heinous sin. Thus the
Jews assumed that they deserved the blessing of the
One who was to come. The Messiah would establish
them as rulers over those who had ruled them.

John the Baptist addressed this misunderstanding:
"And do not think you can say to yourselves 'We
have Abraham as our father.' I tell you that out of
these stones God can raise up children for Abraham"
(Matthew 3:9).

The church today is almost as confused with regard to repentance and contrition as were the people
at the time of John the Baptist. Many assume that re-

pentance is just a one-time acknowledgment of our
naughty nature. But it often ends right there. The
need for a radical change of mind and action is ignored.

Those of us in church leadership are not immune
from this debilitating heresy. Christianity is not
just an intellectual acknowledgment of spiritual
truths. It is about a dramatic change of heart that
alters an entire lifestyle. It is about a whole new attitude of obedience to God's Word and God's will.
Many believers today come to God without any
brokenness and expect to be ushered into the
throne room of His presence without having prepared themselves through mourning or repentance.

A broken lifestyle, a life of contrition grows out of
the awareness that we are indeed "poor in spirit." But
every atom of our being will resist the simple confession that says, "I am a helpless sinner." We desperately want to believe the title of that book from the
'70s, *I'm OK—You're OK.* But I'm *not* OK—and neither are you!

Blessed are those who mourn. We need a fresh understanding of this concept as preparation for leadership and in order to live a godly life. The only way to
become a part of God's kingdom both now and forever is to come to that place where we realize that we
are sinners who are in dire need of a Savior. Then our
wonderful Messiah can deal with past, present and
future iniquity as we cast ourselves completely upon
Him.

All of this prepares us for a life of submission to
God. One of the key benefits of being poor in spirit

and mourning is that it keeps us in a constant state of dependence upon the Lord Jesus. This is absolutely essential in the development of godly character for leadership. Paul put it this way: "What a wretched man I am! Who will rescue me from this body of death? Thanks be to God—through Jesus Christ our Lord!" (Romans 7:24-25).

Apart from Matthew 5:3-4, we will have moral failures, doctrinal heresies and church splits. We tend to focus on the well-publicized disasters of a few high-profile ministries, but the truth is that pastors and church leaders are falling by the wayside in startling numbers. Why? One reason would go back to the necessity for leadership to put *substance of character* before *skills*. We have begun to value charisma over character and the body of Christ has paid a steep price.

Mourning and Joy

David Johnson explains why joy comes when we mourn:

> Joy comes in the mourning. As we deal with our sin, pain and despair, the comfort and grace we receive set the stage for the joy of the Lord in our lives. We may not "feel" it right away. It may not even be an overwhelming emotional ecstasy. But a beautiful joy will settle in over our souls as we experience the relief of getting what's inside to the outside.[2]

Mourning is necessary to our experience so that we understand true joy. Contrition will indeed lead to celebration when it occurs in that order. Too many Christians, however, want the emotional high of happiness first. In Matthew 5, Christ wanted His leaders to understand the concept of "first things first."

Happy is the person who is poor in spirit.

Happy is the person who knows what it is to mourn.

The blessings will come for the humble and contrite.

Brokenness and Relationships

Jesus takes the principle of brokenness through mourning and begins to illustrate how the church leader can apply his personal brokenness to the relationships with those he is responsible to lead. Jesus' expectation is that as the leader changes inside, the way he leads will change also.

The contrite heart is able to deal with anger and manage interpersonal conflicts with others:

> You have heard that it was said to the people long ago, "Do not murder, and anyone who murders will be subject to judgment." But I tell you that anyone who is angry with his brother will be subject to judgment. Again, anyone who says to his brother, "Raca," is answerable to the Sanhedrin. But anyone who says, "You fool!" will be in danger of the fire of hell. (Matthew 5:21-22)

Our Lord was speaking to Jews who did not think they were sinners unless they committed a "big" one like murder. But He points out that we can have a murderous attitude, which, in terms of our relationships with others, can be just as deadly as killing someone.

The word "Raca" means "empty head" and was a common term of derision. The New Living Translation is on target with the translation, "You idiot!" Having such a derogatory attitude toward others shows that we are filled with pride. It is also evidence of the fact that we are not poor in spirit and broken.

A minister friend told me of a frightening experience he had with a summer intern who became irate when given instructions for a task. The young student, who happened to be a large individual, moved toward the senior pastor with a menacing look. He pushed things off the pastor's desk. He began to use vulgar, abusive language. The intern almost took a swing at his mentor before rushing out of the room in a hail of swear words. The anger that surfaced, well out of proportion to the situation, indicated a not-yet-broken area of this man's heart.

Jesus goes right to the heart of a huge problem in the church. Anger is the ultimate tool of Satan to alienate one brother from another in the body of Christ. Animosity always comes loaded with a judgmental spirit: "How could you botch that job so completely?!" This kind of rage is demeaning and destructive of healthy relationships, and has no place in the life of church leaders. This is why the Savior was so blunt in His bold condemnation.

Could there be even one person reading this book who has never been angry with someone else at church? I think not. We are *all* guilty. That is why we must have broken spirits and honest, repentant hearts. We will be better prepared to minister to those in need when we perform a reality check on ourselves in this area of anger. Anger is always a destructive force in relationships.

The man or woman with a broken heart has a new relational perspective. He knows his own struggle with anger and other sins, and realizes that everyone else is operating with the same handicap. Godly leaders don't look down on the flock of Christ as if to say, "Here I am, you lucky sinners!" A gracious tone of humility and brokenness is in every conversation.

Jesus offers the solution for relationships that have been damaged by anger and other offenses:

> Therefore, if you are offering your gift at the altar and there remember that your brother has something against you, leave your gift there in front of the altar. First go and be reconciled to your brother; then come and offer your gift. (Matthew 5:23-24)

Attempted reconciliation is always the action of the broken and contrite heart. Perhaps you noted the use of the word "attempted"? Reconciliation requires more than one person with a contrite spirit. Though I may be willing to reconcile, other people may not be. It is the responsibility of the leader to seek reconciliation; it is the work of the Spirit that accomplishes it. The leader who recognizes his own propensity for sin and truly mourns his corrupt nature will have an attitude that agrees with the songwriter: "Amazing grace, how sweet the sound, that saved a wretch like me." God's broken-hearted servant will not wait for others to come to him. He will seek out those with whom there is conflict and strive for resolution.

It is obvious in this text that serious complications result from the failure to be reconciled with one another. There is no true reconciliation apart from brokenness. Without reconciliation our worship becomes unacceptable to God whether it is in the form of time, talent or treasure. The Lord simply does not want gifts of any kind that are given from those who do not have a clear conscience. God desires a clean heart. This is eloquently expressed in Isaiah:

> "The multitude of your sacrifices—
>   what are they to me?" says the LORD.
> "I have more than enough of burnt
>   offerings,
>   of rams and the fat of fattened animals;
> I have no pleasure
>   in the blood of bulls and lambs
>   and goats.
> When you come to meet with me,
>   who has asked this of you,
>   this trampling of my courts? . . .
> When you spread out your hands in
>   prayer,

> I will hide my eyes from you;
> even if you offer many prayers,
>   I will not listen.
> Your hands are full of blood;
>   wash and make yourselves clean.
> Take your evil deeds
>   out of my sight!
> Stop doing wrong,
>   learn to do right!
> Seek justice,
>   encourage the oppressed.
> Defend the cause of the fatherless,
>   plead the case of the widow.
> "Come now, let us reason together,"
>   says the LORD.
> "Though your sins are like scarlet,
>   they shall be as white as snow;
> though they are red as crimson,
>   they shall be like wool."
>   (Isaiah 1:11-12, 15-18)

The prophet is saying the same thing that Jesus expressed in Matthew 5. The offerings don't really matter because their hearts are full of greed, selfishness and other kinds of unrighteousness. They cannot expect to continue a relationship with God when they were totally incapable of getting along with each other.

The implication for church leaders is crystal clear: God puts a high priority on our relationships with one another. The way we treat each other should reflect the changes that are taking place in our hearts.

As those called to lead the flock model the character quality of brokenness, it will bless others in Christ's body. Joy will come through our mourning.

In this way, leaders can serve, submit to and honor each other as well as those whom they serve. Peter calls us to "clothe [ourselves] with humility toward one another" (1 Peter 5:5). This is in keeping with our Lord's mission statement in Matthew 20:

> You know that the rulers of the Gentiles lord it over them, and their high officials exercise authority over them. Not so with you. Instead, whoever wants to become great among you must be your servant, and whoever wants to be first must be your slave—just as the Son of Man did not come to be served, but to serve, and to give his life as a ransom for many. (Matthew 20:25-28)

This is the essence of Paul's command to "consider others better than yourself" (Philippians 2:3). We are so used to getting our own way and controlling the situation that we trample over the needs of others. We may even be pursuing God's goals, but if we neglect to honor one another in the process, the goal cannot be reached in His way.

Leaders must learn humility in the process of serving the church. A dramatic change of both mind and action will be required to make this happen. But our commitment to Christ and His church requires us to move in the direction of a true brokenness and humility of heart and life.

Blessed are the poor in spirit.

Blessed are those who mourn.

These are the first two foundations for godly leadership—humility that leads to brokenness. But there's more! Read on to discover that "meekness" is *not* synonymous with "weakness."

🏹 LEADERSHIP REFLECTIONS:

1. Personal brokenness and contriteness as leadership characteristics seem a far stretch from most advice on management. Why does Jesus address this in His teaching?
2. Discuss the implications of leaders who are not contrite in their dealings with people.

SUBMISSION

A LEADER DEVELOPS A lifestyle of submission to God which leads to a passion to live God's way. This enables him to live with integrity in all of the relationships of his life.

CHAPTER
THREE

The Strength of Submission

> *Blessed are the meek,*
> *for they will inherit the earth.*
> *(Matthew 5:5)*

One author humorously describes the dilemma suggested by our misconception of "meekness" and Christ's teaching in Matthew 5:5.

Let's pretend you are an employer who is about to conduct an interview with a potential employee. Just before he comes into the room, you glance through his resume and references. One former boss wrote a comment that jumps out at you: "Jim was a good worker and meek." How would that description of a potential employee influence you prior to the interview? Would you be more or less likely to hire a man or woman who is characterized as "meek"? Does this sound like a strong person or a weak one?[1]

For whatever reason, we live in a world that equates *meekness* with *weakness*. The meek soul might be a nice person to have around because they can be pushed around. They would make few, if any, demands. We could easily win arguments with a meek man or woman. But they certainly could not be considered "leadership" material! We want the go-getters. Those adventurous types who know how to assert themselves. *Harvard Business Review* informs us that in the corporate world: "Management controls people by pushing them in the right direction."[2]

Why, then, did Jesus list a submissive spirit as the third character quality of a leader in His kingdom? The Messiah did not refer to concepts like "controlling" and "pushing" people. How could our Lord's ideas be so extremely different?

What must have been going through the minds of the disciples? This great teacher who stood before them was believed by some to be a military leader who would rally the troops for an attack on Rome. The powers that be would be toppled in a show of force. After that conquest, they would rule the world with Christ as their supreme leader.

But then their commander has the audacity to say, "Blessed are the meek." How can a "meek" army overthrow the vast military forces of the Roman Empire? This could turn out to be the shortest battle in history! The disciples must have been bewildered beyond description. Maybe they had made a mistake in signing up with this Messiah. All the flash and sparkle of His miracles were beginning to fade.

Blessed are the meek? It was like dropping a bomb in the middle of this group of hand-picked leaders.

Granted, this was no way to promote yourself as the Messiah. But Jesus said it courageously: Those who treat others with a submissive spirit will be happy and fulfilled. Those who submit to God with a humble, broken spirit will be blessed. Those who want to lead His kingdom people must have these character qualities.

Understanding Meekness

Let's seek a better understanding of this concept of meekness or submission as described by our Savior. The Greek word for "meek" is *praos*. Its root meaning is "gentle, mild or tender." In classical Greek, it was used to describe a soothing medicine or a gentle breeze. One might even suggest a translation such as, "Blessed are those whose spirits produce a soothing medicine and a gentle breeze in their leadership relationships." Kingdom leaders— true kingdom leaders—are like that.

But even classical Greek cannot give the full meaning of Jesus' use of this word in its context. In using this word, Jesus was insisting that His leaders' character would be distinguished by a truly meek, submissive spirit that overcomes haughtiness and arrogance in relationships with those we serve and lead.

We in the church have a tendency to equate leadership with power and authority rather than service. Jesus began to address this misconception when He described this leadership prerequisite of meekness. Meekness or a submissive spirit is about our relationship with God, but it has a direct consequence in our relationships with those we serve. How many stories have you heard (and never repeated of course) of those who have gone to church leaders with a concern only to have their concern explained away as unjust and irrelevant? Submissive leaders are listening leaders who, like Jesus, always seek God's perspective on issues and concerns rather than pressing on with their own agendas.

Many churches seem to be organized more according to the principles of the *world* than those of the *Word*. We get caught up in persuasive power, elaborate organizational structures and legalistic judgments. It is sometimes a vivid demonstration of what human beings can produce apart from God. This may be interesting, but it cannot be anointed. It may produce a lot of *action*, but it will lack the one thing that enables it to change the world: *unction*.

God blesses the leader who is truly submissive. Profoundly simple. Simply profound. And all of the showmanship that any church can muster with elegant music, drama, strict rules or eloquent teaching will never amount to anything of eternal value apart from this teaching of Christ.

The Lifestyle of Submission

The meek are those kingdom people who no longer trust in themselves. They do not rely on their own powers or abilities. They have submitted themselves to God. In relating to others this submitted servant becomes a representative of the Lord Himself—a servant leader. This is the result of seeing that they have nothing to offer God in terms of their own righteous-ness. In the words of John the Baptist, "He must be-come greater; I must become less" (John 3:30).

God is supremely interested in our personal sub-mission to Him. This lifestyle is essential to any leadership role we may have in a small or large church. It is more vital than any award or recogni-tion we might receive for serving Him. It is so easy to get caught up in the numbers game and assume that if "big" things are happening, we must be walk-ing closely with the Lord. The Bible offers the story of Gideon to highlight God's priority for submis-sive servants.

Gideon did not exactly have the kind of résumé that would recommend him as a brave, accomplished soldier. In fact, we are introduced to him as a coward who is hiding from the Midianites. He is crouched in the bottom of a winepress to conceal the wheat that he was threshing. God sent an angel to say to this frightened man, "The LORD is with you, mighty war-rior" (Judges 6:12).

Gideon must have looked around for a moment before realizing that the angel was speaking to him. He did not feel like much of a "mighty warrior" as he took cover in the winepress. It took a while for the angel to convince Gideon that he was indeed God's chosen leader for the army of Israel. He felt handi-capped by two things: first, his clan was the weakest of all the clans in the tribe of Manasseh; second, of his own family, he was the last one to be chosen for leadership of any kind. (Think "David" just before Goliath was rocked to sleep.)

But the bottom line was that Gideon had submitted his life and times to Jehovah. When it became clear to him that God was speaking through the angel, he was ready to become that "mighty hero," a leader of God's people. So, in Gideon's mind, the next step was to amass a huge army that could overwhelm any force. Then the Lord made this startling announcement: "Gideon, you need to downsize. You have too many warriors with you" (see Judges 7:2).

Before it was all over, God had ordered his army reduced from 32,000 soldiers to 300—slightly less than 1 percent of the original fighting force. Though we have no record of Gideon objecting to this massive reduction, he must have wondered how the Lord was going to pull this off. But he was controlled by a submissive spirit; he proceeded to do God's work in God's way, and the battle was over in a few short hours.

Why did the Lord downsize Gideon's troops so dramatically? If this leader had defeated the Midianites with a large army, he would have been tempted to take all or some of the credit for utilizing clever military tactics. But a war won with a mere 300 men left only one person to be praised for the victory: God Himself. The Lord wanted Gideon to know that he was a "mighty hero" only because "The Lord is with you."

Paul expresses this valuable lesson in these words:

> But God chose the foolish things of the world to shame the wise; God chose the

> weak things of the world to shame the strong. He chose the lowly things of this world and the despised things—and the things that are not—to nullify the things that are, so that no one may boast before him. (1 Corinthians 1:27-29)

How desperately we need to get a handle on the Apostle Paul's words as he describes how God does things. It seems so upside down, so backwards, so non-human. Yes! It is supernatural, God-centered. This is the kind of person, the kind of leader, Christ is seeking.

He is looking for leaders in His kingdom work who have learned the lessons of true humility. He needs men and women with broken hearts. He wants those who are totally submitted to His will and His way. God does not primarily need our clever organizational skills. He wants to use our abilities only as they are submitted to Him in the context of His character. He does not require money or famous people to get the job done, though he may use money and the famous if they are humble, broken, submissive men and women who will simply say with Gideon, "God, I'll do it *Your* way."

Complete Submission

In Romans 12, Paul reminds us that we are called to a total abandonment of ourselves to the Lord:

> Therefore, I urge you, brothers, in view of God's mercy, to offer your bodies as living sacrifices, holy and pleasing to God—this is

> your spiritual act of worship. Do not con-
> form any longer to the pattern of this world,
> but be transformed by the renewing of your
> mind. Then you will be able to test and ap-
> prove what God's will is—his good, pleasing
> and perfect will. (Romans 12:1-2)

This passage attacks one of our greatest fears—the loss of personal control. We do not want to surrender the management of our lives to anyone else—not even God Himself. But the Lord wants *all* of you and *all* of me. By using the phrase "give your bodies," the apostle was calling for a complete surrender.

Paul uses a strange phrase to describe the nature of this submission: a *living sacrifice*. This is God's way of saying that He wants us both "dead" and "alive." We need to be willing to "die" to our self-ishness and self-centered lifestyle while at the same time being "alive" to Christlikeness. And this is the only reasonable response to the great sacrifice Jesus made on our behalf. It is the only reasonable manner in which to lead Christ's church.

This kind of meek, submissive attitude is a moral necessity for every pastor and church leader. It will need to be developed over a lifetime of radical commitment. No one will ever be able to say, "Well, I've finally learned all there is to know about meekness and submission." Even the most seasoned saints will need to come back again and again to this principle.

The wonderful result of living a Romans 12:1 lifestyle is that we will be transformed (12:2). We will be thrust into what could be called a "state of change."

We will continually be changing to conform to the image of Christ. As we move away from the behavior and customs of this world, we will develop a new way of thinking. New attitudes and values—His very character—will begin to be formed within us.

With a clear, cleansed mind, we will be able to discern the Lord's will for those that we lead: "Then you will be able to test and approve what God's will is—his good, pleasing and perfect will" (Romans 12:2). Many pastors and leaders in the church are in a fog for this very reason. Proud, self-centered leaders cannot clearly see what the Lord has in store for them or His church. His plan is reserved for humble, broken, meek servants. Theirs is the kingdom of heaven. We need to know what He is doing so we can in submission line up our activities with what He is doing in our town, community and church.

Submission and Relationships

Jesus offers some pointed illustrations of the principle surrounding "Blessed are the meek." The issues He raises include some of the most difficult leadership issues that must be faced in the church today—adultery and divorce. Bear in mind that Christ is demonstrating how a lack of submission to God can lead to rampant selfishness. This is the root cause of both adultery and divorce.

> You have heard that it was said, "Do not commit adultery." But I tell you that anyone who looks at a woman lustfully has already committed adultery with her in his heart. . . . It has been said, "Anyone who

divorces his wife must give her a certificate
of divorce." But I tell you that anyone who
divorces his wife, except for marital un-
faithfulness, causes her to become an adul-
teress, and anyone who marries the
divorced woman commits adultery. (Matthew 5:27-28, 31-32)

The emphasis here is similar to that in Romans 12.
A disciple (and a leader must first be a disciple) must
submit his entire body and mind to the Lord. If we do
not surrender ourselves in this fashion, we open our
lives up to every imaginable kind of carnal passion.
Sexual sins will then lead to broken marriage cove-
nants, divorce and untold pain and heartache for
both partners and their extended families. But keep
in mind where it all started: resisting the lifestyle of
meekness and submission to God.

Adultery and divorce are two of the hottest topics
of debate in the modern church, much as they were
in the time of Christ. How can a pastor and his leaders make tough decisions in this regard apart from
humility, brokenness and total submission to the
Lord? We can reduce the rhetoric surrounding these
explosive issues only as we demonstrate that we have
been broken at the cross. Then we can proceed to
point out the need for others to embrace Romans
12:1-2.

Submission and Integrity

Again, you have heard that it was said to
the people long ago, "Do not break your
oath, but keep the oaths you have made to

the Lord." But I tell you, Do not swear at all: either by heaven, for it is God's throne; or by the earth, for it is his footstool. . . . Simply let your "Yes," be "Yes," and your "No," "No"; anything beyond this comes from the evil one. (Matthew 5:33-35, 37)

Christ offers another illustration of practical ways we can demonstrate our submission to God and one another. Moses had to deal with leaders in Israel who had developed an elaborate and complicated system of vows which allowed them to be deceitful. So the old covenant law taught that the people were not to make promises that they could not keep. Vows made to God were particularly binding.

At the time of our Lord, the Pharisees and teachers of the law had made things even more complicated. Jesus knew that the only way to deal with this tangled web was to abolish it entirely and get back to basics. A paraphrase of His teaching would look like this: "When you say 'yes,' mean it. When you say 'no,' mean it."

The truly meek person does not want to deceive in any way. He or she wants to be up-front and easy to understand. In this way, pastors and leaders need to be men and women of the highest integrity. False and misleading statements must be rejected and replaced with a commitment to tell the truth, the whole truth, and nothing but the truth.

Submission and Rights

Christ had some challenging things to say to the Pharisees with regard to revenge:

> You have heard that it was said, "Eye for
> eye, and tooth for tooth." But I tell you, Do
> not resist an evil person. If someone strikes
> you on the right cheek, turn to him the
> other also. And if someone wants to sue you
> and take your tunic, let him have your cloak
> as well. If someone forces you to go one
> mile, go with him two miles. Give to the one
> who asks you, and do not turn away from
> the one who wants to borrow from you.
> (Matthew 5:38-42)

When Jesus is Lord in your life, you will put
other people first. This is another facet of the principle of meekness: Put others before yourself and
God will take care of you.

This seemed a bit radical for the religious leaders of
Christ's day. They were in love with the Old Testament
idea that if you poke my eye, I will poke yours. If you
break my tooth, you can count on a right hook to your
jaw, too. At all costs, the spirit of retaliation had to be
satisfied. This was the way it was meant to be and the
Pharisees, scribes and teachers of the law were in no
mood to change. It sounds like society today, where
me, myself and I—my rights—reign supreme.

But the Messiah offered a radical alternative. In
His kingdom, retribution is replaced with submission, forgiveness and love. He illustrates this in four
ways:

1. Turn the other cheek to be slapped
2. Give up your coat as well as your shirt
3. Go two miles when asked to go just one

4. Instead of avoiding those who want to borrow from you, help them out.

"Turning the other cheek" requires a healthy dose of dying to self. No one wants to be insulted or slapped around. I discovered how difficult this can be driving home one evening from work. It was 5:45 p.m. I had several miles to go and I was already fifteen minutes late for dinner. The street was jammed with traffic. Every time I tried to switch lanes, someone would cut me off. I remember thinking to myself in utter frustration, "Why is everyone else trying to go the same direction I am going at the same time I need to get there?"

The Lord asked me a question as I sat paralyzed in the congestion: "What were you thinking when those people wouldn't let you into their lane?" I immediately knew the answer: I couldn't wait to *cut them off* when I got the chance! I was very much caught up in the mentality of "an eye for an eye, and a tooth for a tooth."

Kingdom living challenges us to die to this selfish passion to exalt self and obtain revenge. When someone does us intentional wrong and we can respond in love, recognizing who they are in Christ apart from their own behavior, then we are truly submitted. We are obviously talking about the supernatural power of God in our lives to react in this manner. The human reaction is to retaliate at the first opportunity.

This is a powerful role model for church leadership to offer. Think about a church board meeting.

Someone lashes out in a personal attack on the pastor or an elder. A demonstration of meekness on the part of the one being assailed will set a tremendous example for the others. Does this mean that the brother or sister who lashed out should not be held accountable for their loss of control? No! Leaders should take up this matter with the offending party. But the one who was under attack can enjoy the victory of Christ over his tendency to fight back.

If we have truly embraced what it means to be poor in spirit, broken and submissive, it does not really matter how people treat us. We must die to the spirit of resentment and demonstrate a servant attitude as leaders. This demeanor is very attractive and compelling. Others will want to follow this kind of leader.

Martin Lloyd-Jones tells the story about Billy Bray, the famous Cornish evangelist who was a boxer prior to his conversion. Shortly after he was saved, he was working in the mines. A man who had previously feared Mr. Bray thought that this might be a good time to test his Christianity.

> Without any provocation at all he struck Billy Bray, who could have very easily revenged himself upon him. . . . But instead of doing that, Billy Bray looked at him and said, "May God forgive you, even as I have forgiven you." . . . The result was that this man endured for several days an agony of

mind and spirit which led directly to his conversion.[3]

Loving the Enemy

Next, Christ calls for the internalization of the principle of submission to be expressed in the ultimate manner of loving those who hate us:

> You have heard that it was said, "Love your neighbor and hate your enemy." But I tell you: Love your enemies and pray for those who persecute you. . . . If you love those who love you, what reward will you get? Are not even the tax collectors doing that? And if you greet only your brothers, what are you doing more than others? Do not even pagans do that? Be perfect, therefore, as your heavenly Father is perfect. (Matthew 5:43-44, 46-48)

What a fanatical concept! It is one thing to tell people to love their neighbors. It is quite another thing to instruct them to love an *enemy* and pray for a *persecutor*! As a standard for church leadership, this raises the bar considerably. We must get beyond the comfort zone of loving those who are supportive and kind to us. Our love must extend to those who have intentionally chosen to be against us.

When a pastor first arrives at a church, an enemy or two will often surface in the first weeks or months of his ministry. This may or may not be related to a particular offense that was committed. Some folks have chosen to be *every* pastor's adversary. A minister friend told me of an elder in a southern state who said to the new pastor: "I've gotten rid of six preachers before you and I can get rid of you, too!"

Anyone who is truly a leader and is serving in a leadership position will have enemies. There are carnal, self-serving people who will not respond to leadership of any kind and who will rise up and become enemies of pastors and other church leaders. For example, recently I have seen churches where a staff member spent much time and effort undercutting the senior pastor in order to usurp his position. In one situation the usurper was eventually successful and served in the senior pastor role for a short period of time. (Though many lay people may not be aware of it, these kinds of stories are unfortunately all too common; they are a staple of discussion at many pastoral meetings.)

Even though I and others have been deeply hurt by this kind of action, our responsibility is to love that staff person with Christ's love. Let me assure you it does not happen overnight. Nonetheless our behavior and decisions must reflect Christ's love. This will keep us from falling into bitterness and sin. Many of us have learned the hard way that being submitted to Christ as a leader does not always mean the simple path, but God's way is best. Submission does not necessarily change the circumstances but it can change us into leaders who have learned how to love and forgive those who chose to be our enemies.

So it's not a question of *if* spiritual leaders will encounter enemies, but *when*. After that, the most important issue is how that leader responds to the antagonist. Here is our Lord's answer (my para-phrase): "Blessed are those who are submitted, for the whole earth will belong to them (even when it does not feel that way)." This is the strength of sub-mission! Only when you are walking under authority are you able to exercise the grace and mercy of God's authority. Godly leaders can model humility, broken-ness and meekness by loving the very enemies who enjoy persecuting them!

This is what distinguishes the committed disciple of Christ from the rest of the population. We can love those who gossip about us. We can love those who are trying to get our job or our promotion. We can love those who constantly irritate us. As we do this, we are demonstrating to all that there is a higher plane of living which calls for higher character. And all of this is possible only through the indwelling Christ.

Jesus concludes Matthew 5 by noting that all of this is the beginning of being perfect "even as your Father in heaven is perfect." Perfection is simply living in obedience to the Word of God in every area that He is presently addressing in our lives. This does not mean that He will not continue to show us new areas—indeed, He will! But to be con-sidered "perfect" from God's perspective, we need to be honestly and openly dealing with all sin He has revealed to this point. This is the commitment to a meek, submitted life in the Lord.

Such radical submission to God and His way leads us to submit to one another—even those who have set themselves up to be our enemies. And character like this builds leaders—Christlike leaders.

Humility. Brokenness. Submission. These are the first three traits of godly leadership. The next character quality continues this theme of being "perfected."

🚩 LEADERSHIP REFLECTIONS

1. We live in a world where submission is low on the list of character qualities. How does a submissive attitude reflect itself in your leadership relationships?
2. Discuss the issues of submission and rights, integrity and how we relate to those we lead. What other passages of Scripture reflect on this subject?

DEPENDENCE

THE LEADER MUST BE hungering and thirsting after righteousness. As he does, he will be filled. This dependence on Christ will lead to new attitudes toward service, forgiveness and personal stewardship.

CHAPTER

FOUR

In Dependence

*Blessed are those who hunger and
thirst for righteousness,
for they will be filled.*

(Matthew 5:6)

ost of us think we can relate to the
concept of being hungry or thirsty.
But in North America, where food and
water are generally plentiful, we need to expand our
thinking to have an idea of what this Beatitude
means. A coach with a team in last place may be hungry for a win. Someone may be very thirsty for en-
couragement or a compliment. In whatever arena,
hunger is a state of mind that is very possessive. We
will do just about anything to have our need satisfied.

The Palestinians were particularly tuned to Jesus'
reference to hunger and thirst. For many in this culture, starvation was but a day or two away. Dehy-
dration was just around the corner. Most of us
think of "hunger" or "thirst" in terms of going without food or drink for a few hours. But Jesus' followers knew the genuine pangs of deprivation. When
He said, "Blessed are those who hunger and thirst,"
they could relate.

So Jesus uses this illustration from daily life to describe the next character quality. The disciples have been blown away by the principles of humility, brokenness and submission. Now we come to blockbuster number four: A godly leader is one who is constantly dependent on the Lord.

"Blessed are those who hunger and thirst for righteousness." This is a reference to the continual process of being filled with the Spirit of God. He makes us aware of our poverty of spirit, our need to be broken and totally submissive to His will. This requires the steady flow of His life and virtue into our lives—we will be forever dependent on Him.

Many believers make the mistake of thinking that their conversion experience was the end. In actuality, it was the beginning. It was the start of a whole new way of life, a new relationship. We do not arrive when we are saved. Instead, we have entered the door to a lifelong process of getting to know the Lord Jesus more fully. After several years of walking with God, Paul humbly admits:

> Not that I have already obtained all this, or have already been made perfect, but I press on to take hold of that for which Christ Jesus took hold of me. Brothers, I do not consider myself yet to have taken hold of it. But one thing I do: Forgetting what is behind and straining toward what is ahead, I press on . . . (Philippians 3:12-14)

In chapters 5-8 of this book, we will discover where this pursuit of God is leading us that we might lead others. As we seek to know Christ in His fullness, He will produce in us:

- a merciful character (Matthew 5:7) . . . so we can lead mercifully
- a pure heart (5:8) . . . so we can lead with holiness
- a passion to be a peacemaker (5:9) . . . so we can lead in peace
- a character to withstand persecution (5:10-12) . . . so we can lead in the midst of turmoil.

The result of this journey will be a deeper love and relationship with the Lord so we can lead as He would lead. We will have a sharper awareness of His Spirit within and see evidence of His fruit without. Any attempt at church leadership that does not focus on this all-out pursuit of God and His righteousness will lead to personal disaster as well as dysfunction in the body of Christ. Leaders tend to reproduce, in their ministries, their own values and strengths—as well as their weaknesses. As we demonstrate a pursuit of God and His righteousness the church will follow.

This takes us back to some of my thoughts in the introduction. Many churches are not seeing growth by conversion because we have either ignored or rejected the Savior's seminar on spiritual leadership in Matthew 5! We have resisted His teaching in favor of copying the guys we think are doing it well, rather than seeking what God is doing where we are and getting in the midst of His work of righteousness. The results have been catastrophic and counterproductive to God's kingdom purposes.

In the Sermon on the Mount, we discover tenets that represent *internal character traits* that can only be obtained through the supernatural process prescribed by our Lord and Savior. There are no gimmicks here. Christ does not offer *Three Steps to Building the Biggest Church in Town*. He insisted that character and skills are intertwined in the church. Skill apart from character may build the "biggest" but it may not be "His best." The practical conclusion we come to as church leaders is that if we have a choice in leaders of skill with little character or character with little skill we should always, *always* go with character and help them learn the skills.

Emptied to Be Filled

Church leadership must come from those who are undergoing a revolutionary change of character. As they are humbled, broken and submissive, a vacuum is formed. And it can only be meaningfully filled by the Spirit of God and His righteousness.

This is essentially why all of us need to be shaken out of our comfort and complacency. It is easy to fall into the trap of believing that we are righteous enough to be independent of God and His supply. But in His great grace, He allows the circumstances of our lives to bring us to this point of complete dependence on the Lord.

A minister friend had a traumatic experience that many church leaders seem to encounter at some point in their pilgrimage. He and his wife were interviewed by a church that was hundreds of miles from their present parish. During the candidating process, every sign seemed to be pointing in that direction. After receiving what had been reported as a unanimous call from the governing board, the pastor accepted.

Two months after they had arrived, it became clear that they had been completely deceived during the interview process. The same board that had heartily agreed to his vision for the church began to turn against him. Vicious gossip and slander began to swirl around the congregation like a tornado. After just four months, this minister and his family had to move back to the same town from which they had come.

Although the months and years that followed were challenging in many ways, the pastor told me that he learned one major lesson: We need to be empty before God can fill us. This dear brother had enjoyed success throughout his ministry, but the Lord used this humbling, breaking experience to deepen his sense of submission to, and dependence on, Jesus Christ. He learned in more intimate ways what it means to "hunger and thirst for righteousness alone."

Hungry for What?

As a follower of Christ and a church leader, we must ask a crucial question: "What is the one thing that consumes the majority of my time, thinking and resources?" When we truthfully answer this inquiry, that "one thing" will be the object of our hunger and thirst. Unfortunately, the answer may not be "the righteousness of God."

We may be hungering and thirsting after material things—a bigger house, a better boat, a newer car. We could have a passion for the praise of others. This is what drives many to work long hours overtime. We might devote ourselves to sensual pleasures. There are so many things that can captivate our hearts.

Some pastors and church leaders get caught up in get-rich-quick schemes and end up exploiting the very people they are supposed to be helping. The church becomes a place to cultivate customers and sell services. It can begin innocently with even a hint of ministry. But it often ends with people in the congregation feeling like they have been conned.

Godly leaders are called to focus their time, thinking and resources on the righteousness of God. This is to be our all-consuming desire. Righteousness is a craving to be free from sin in all of its manifestations. As we realize that sin alone keeps us from really knowing the Lord, we long to be liberated from evil.

However, we must recognize there are differing perspectives that pass for righteousness in the church. Jesus refers to the "righteousness . . . of the Pharisees" in Matthew 5:20 as a self-centered, behavior-measured kind of living that passed for the casual observer as true righteousness. Their external behavior seemed to fit the rules (rules they had made) and they attended all the right seminars, but . . .

In contrast, Philippians 3:9 speaks of Christ's righteousness, which is internal. It starts from within and causes behavior that is consistent with the Word of God. Its goal is not applause but obedience. This keeps us looking to Jesus and relying on Him. If we were capable of producing our own holiness, we would not need to be poor in spirit, mourning our sinfulness, meek or dependent. In the words of Paul, "I consider them rubbish [those things I have lost], that I may gain Christ and be found in him, not having a righteousness of my own that comes from the law, but that which is through faith in Christ" (Philippians 3:8-9).

Freedom from the Power of Sin

Pursuing righteousness is not only the desire to be free from the *penalty of sin*. It is also the passion to be emancipated from the *powerful grip of sin* in our lives. Paul talked openly about this problem and its solution:

> For when we were controlled by the sinful nature, the sinful passions aroused by the law were at work in our bodies, so that we bore fruit for death. But now, by dying to what once bound us, we have been released from the law so that we serve in the new way of the Spirit, and not in the old way of the written code. (Romans 7:5-6)

Pastors and church leaders need to be aware of the enormous power of sin in their own lives as well as the lives of those they serve. But they must also realize that the divine energy generated by the death and resurrection of Christ is more than a match for the strength of the old nature. Even the carnal nature combined with all the powers of darkness cannot come close to the force unleashed at the empty tomb. The apostle celebrates this in Romans 6 and 8:

> For we know that our old self was cruci-
> fied with him so that the body of sin might
> be done away with, that we should no lon-
> ger be slaves to sin—because anyone who
> has died has been freed from sin. . . .
> Therefore, there is now no condemnation
> for those who are in Christ Jesus, because
> through Christ Jesus the law of the Spirit
> of life set me free from the law of sin and
> death. (Romans 6:6-7, 8:1-2)

We have a whole new existence because of the cross-work of Christ. We can walk in newness of life because we have repented of our sins, humbled ourselves, submitted ourselves to God and sought His righteousness. We have hungered and thirsted after His holiness because we knew that without it we simply could not live. This has liberated us from the cruel tyranny of the sin nature in our lives.

No longer do we need to say, "What a wretched man I am!" (Romans 7:24). We do not have to keep on sinning as a way of life because Christ is greater than the flesh and the devil. Jesus can live in and through our human bodies to give glory to His Father. This is the blessedness of God's righteousness—freedom from being forced to sin by the old Adamic nature—freedom to live a life that pleases our Lord.

If all of this is true—and it is—then why do we continue in sin? The answer is simple, but embarrassing. We enjoy it. There is a certain element of pleasure in iniquity. In the process of time, Christ wants to overhaul our desires so that our passion to please Him outweighs any perceived joys or benefits derived from sinning. As we begin to abhor those transgressions, we will confess them to God and choose not to live under their power any longer. When we have truly repented, we can instantly claim His forgiveness, cleansing and power to resist the temptation to do the same thing again.

Ultimately, this is a battle with the old self-life. We cannot conquer the carnal nature through some magical potion or prayer. *Jesus has already won that victory*. We simply need to claim it and believe it with all of our hearts. By faith, we accept the completed work of our Savior and move on. Recognition of this battle in us as leaders should give us compassion in dealing with the sins of others in the congregation. At the same time as we call ourselves to the holiness of His righteousness, we must also call those we are leading.

A Three-Ring Circus

In Matthew 6, Jesus warns of the wrong kind of righteousness among those who claimed to be spiritual leaders: "Be careful not to do your 'acts of righteousness' before men, to be seen by them. If you do, you will have no reward from your Father in heaven" (Matthew 6:1).

There is a little "showman" in all of us. When we do something kind or generous, we want to be noticed. If you don't believe this, see what happens the next time you forget to publicly thank someone who helped with the annual Christmas pageant!

Deep inside, all of us—especially leaders—want to be considered "spiritual." It is the ultimate compliment. On occasion, I have been introduced as a "man of God," and I must say that I like the label! But Christ offers a reality check here. Just whose righteousness is it anyway? Does anyone really have room to boast in His presence? Evidently not. God will take away the reward of any person who tries to create them for himself.

The story is told of an elder who approached his pastor shortly after his term had ended on the governing board. He said, "Pastor, I'd sure love to be considered for the position of 'Elder Emeritus.' Would you pray about that?" The minister had to politely deny the request. According to kingdom standards, he had removed himself from consideration by asking for the honor.

The Pharisees celebrated this same kind of external spirituality. Their righteousness was not rooted in a supernatural, internal change. It did not spring forth from a sincere hunger and thirst for God Himself to fill their souls. The pseudo-holiness of these pseudo-leaders was all about outward behaviors that would impress their followers. In truth, they were hollow on the inside.

The message to church leaders today is plain: the Lord wants to build substance and godly character from the inside out. This righteousness is not something we put on like a new suit. It must come from within in order to be characterized as the holiness of Christ.

The Silent Offering

Jesus illustrated this when He addressed the matter of benevolent giving to the needy:

> So when you give to the needy, do not announce it with trumpets, as the hypocrites do in the synagogues and on the streets, to be honored by men. I tell you the truth, they have received their reward in full. But when you give to the needy, do not let your left hand know what your right hand is doing, so that your giving may be in secret. Then your Father, who sees what is done in secret, will reward you. (Matthew 6:2-4)

Some background here is helpful. The tradition of the wealthy men of that day was to announce their offerings with great pomp and circumstance. They would load their camels, dress themselves in fancy purple and golden garments and then come to town with loud trumpets blaring to proclaim their wonderful generosity.

Christ was saying in essence, "Put away your trumpets and use them for worship. But when you give offerings, do so out of your love for God and worship Him. Don't do it just to be seen." Jesus proclaims that His Father will "reward" that kind of unpretentious giving. This does not mean that the Lord will return to you whatever you give in a monetary sense.

But we will be repaid again and again with His honor and righteousness.

A friend of mine told me about a simple way to practice Matthew 6:3. At Christmastime, his family chooses a needy individual or family to help. They find a "middleman" who will deliver the cash gift to this family while the identity of the donor remains anonymous. He simply says, "Someone wanted you to have a very merry Christmas. God bless you."

The important principle here is that our righteousness in helping others should not be motivated by others being able to see it. It should, instead, be motivated by God's love.

The Privacy of Prayer

Christ continues to describe the kind of righteousness we should hunger and thirst for by talking about the right kind of praying:

> And when you pray, do not be like the hypocrites, for they love to pray standing in the synagogues and on the street corners to be seen by men. I tell you the truth, they have received their reward in full. But when you pray, go into your room, close the door and pray to your Father, who is unseen. Then your Father, who sees what is done in secret, will reward you. And when you pray, do not keep on babbling like pagans, for they think they will be heard because of their many words. Do not be like them, for your Father knows what you need before you ask him. (Matthew 6:5-8)

Again we see that the motive of the Pharisees with regard to prayer was impure. They prayed in public, offering long supplications in order to be seen and heard. A modern illustration of this kind of vanity would be a person who loudly yawns throughout the day while announcing to anyone who will listen, "I was up early praying several hours this morning." This has nothing whatsoever to do with hungering and thirsting after righteousness.

Jesus also points out that repeating the same old prayers over and over again is not a sign of deep spirituality. We are to talk to the Lord out of a genuine need, with praise in our hearts. We can develop a relationship with Almighty God the same way we would become friends with another human being—by sharing openly and honestly with Him. In the verses that follow, Jesus offers an example of this kind of honest communication with God:

> Our Father in heaven,
> hallowed be your name,
> your kingdom come,
> your will be done
>   on earth as it is in heaven.
> Give us today our daily bread.
> Forgive us our debts,
>   as we also have forgiven our debtors.
> And lead us not into temptation,
> but deliver us from the evil one. (Matthew 6:9-13)

Forgiving Others

Another aspect of the righteousness which grows out of our hearts is in the act of forgiving others: "For if you forgive men when they sin against you, your heavenly Father will also forgive you. But if you do not forgive men their sins, your Father will not forgive your sins" (Matthew 6:14-15).

This teaching follows immediately after the instruction on prayer. We are to seek God's forgiveness for our own sins based on the fact that we have shown mercy toward those who have offended us. But if we cannot forgive others, we have no basis to expect pardon from the Lord. Forgiveness and restoration must be a two-way street.

Church leaders must be on guard with this issue. Our cynical society claims their right to be victims— angry, bitter and unforgiving. The damage done to people who cannot forgive others is inestimable. But the fact that we struggle with this in the house of God is unconscionable; we should know better.

The victim mentality seduces us into believing that because someone has mistreated us, we have a legitimate reason to resent him and retaliate against the offender. No such right exists. The Savior bluntly states that we will be the recipients of God's grace and forgiveness to the same degree that we offer it to those who hurt us. Leaders in tune with the Holy Spirit will be sensitive to this important reality.

All too often we hear of people who attend the same church but cannot talk with each other "just because." Years of fellowship are lost because someone did or said something that created a barrier of bitterness. Pastors and church leaders must deal with any issues in their own lives in this regard. Only then will they be able to effectively minister healing to the broken relationships in the fellowship.

Comb Your Hair and Wash Your Face

How does righteousness appear in the person who is fasting? Take a look:

> When you fast, do not look somber as the hypocrites do, for they disfigure their faces to show men they are fasting. I tell you the truth, they have received their reward in full. But when you fast, put oil on your head and wash your face, so that it will not be obvious to men that you are fasting, but only to you Father, who is unseen; and your Father, who sees what is done in secret, will reward you. (Matthew 6:16-18)

Blessed are those who hunger and thirst after righteousness. But what kind of righteousness? In this text, Christ says *not* the kind that wants to show off its spiritual discipline! We are not to fast so that others will be greatly impressed with our devout spirituality. Along with the other devotional practices, fasting should be done discreetly as a demonstration of our hunger to know God better and see His will accomplished.

Do other people really need to know how long we pray and study the Word, or how much we give, or how often we attend church? Not really. These are private aspects of our relationship with the Lord that should remain confidential. The temptation to display our dedication arises from the carnal nature and its desire to receive glory and honor.

An Impossible Standard

It becomes clear that Jesus is upping the ante in this matter of spiritual character for those who would be leaders in His church. And the higher that standard goes, the more we recognize our inability to attain this level of holiness. However, this can yield a positive result: we become more dependent on the Lord.

As we look back at several illustrations that the Savior has used, it is remarkable how they were aimed at so-called spiritual leaders who were enamored by their own self-righteousness. Consider some of the ways Christ proved that the Pharisees and Scribes were unable to keep the law:

- "Do not murder." The Pharisees could pull this one off in their own strength. But when the Messiah said that hatred and ridicule would place you in danger of hell, they could not measure up.

- They could abide by the law that said, "Do not commit adultery." However, when Christ insisted that lusting was infidelity of the heart, the bar was again raised too high for them.

- These blind leaders loved the old saying, "An eye for an eye and a tooth for a tooth."

They could do that. But when Jesus challenged them to turn the other cheek and go
the second mile, the command went beyond
their personal abilities.

- "Love your neighbor and hate your enemy"
seemed easy enough to obey. So Christ took it
up a notch by directing them to love their *enemies* and praying for those who *persecuted* them!

Was Jesus being cruel by setting standards that
were impossible to attain? Not at all. He was simply
raising the standard to remind us that it is not I, but
Christ in me who meets the standard. Dependency
on Him and His righteousness is the ultimate in
freedom as we lead. Not I—but the living creator of
all—wants to lead through me. But only as I am
willing to die to self, to be submitted to Him and to
walk in His righteousness.

How can the church be best led? With broken
leaders and dependent followers! We need men and
women who are dying the death of self and living the
life of Christ! We need pastors, elders and board
members who have been humbled by their own inability to obey God in the energy of the flesh. These
are the kinds of leaders who will shake a lost and
lonely community for the kingdom of God.

The God of Money

Christ's leadership workshop continues with an
issue that is sticky for everyone: the struggle with
materialism. Jesus says:

> Do not store up for yourselves treasures
> on earth, where moth and rust destroy,

> and where thieves break in and steal. But
> store up for yourselves treasures in heaven,
> where moth and rust do not destroy, and
> where thieves do not break in and steal.
> For where your treasure is, there your
> heart will be also.
>
> The eye is the lamp of the body. If your
> eyes are good, your whole body will be full
> of light. But if your eyes are bad, your
> whole body will be full of darkness. If then
> the light within you is darkness, how great
> is that darkness!
>
> No one can serve two masters. Either he
> will hate the one and love the other, or he
> will be devoted to the one and despise the
> other. You cannot serve both God and
> Money. (Matthew 6:19-24)

Here is the warning of this passage: if materialism
gains a stronghold in our hearts, it will blur our spiritual
vision. This is a particularly potent illustration for any
of us who have worn contact lenses that were not quite
right. It is an extremely frustrating dilemma! The eyes
will not focus and we are unable to see clearly. This is
precisely what happens when people get caught up in
money and the things it can buy. Paul echoes this senti-
ment in his first letter to Timothy:

> People who want to get rich fall into temp-
> tation and a trap and into many foolish and
> harmful desires that plunge men into ruin
> and destruction. For the love of money is a
> root of all kinds of evil. Some people, eager

for money, have wandered from the faith and pierced themselves with many griefs. (1 Timothy 6:9-10)

To understand the word "treasure" as Christ used it in Matthew 6, suppose that you had a disease and the doctor concluded that you had four weeks to live. When two weeks had gone by, you were informed of a cure for your illness that is ninety-nine percent certain. However, the cost of that procedure would require you to liquidate everything you own—your home, your car, your furniture—everything but the clothes on your back. In addition, you must get the maximum loan available from your bank. Would you go to these extreme lengths to be cured? I would. And I think you would, too.

"Treasures" are those things we would *not* be willing to liquidate in order to meet the need of *someone else* in the body of Christ. They are of such value to us that we would not be willing to share them even if someone else's life was on the line. This goes to the very heart of independent selfishness. Christ is looking for men and women who will gladly surrender even their most treasured possessions to help someone else or to further the cause of His kingdom.

A.W. Tozer gives us the background on our love affair with "things":

Before the Lord God made man upon the earth, He first prepared for him a world of useful and pleasant things for his sustenance and delight. In the Genesis account of the creation these are simply called "things." They were made for man's use, but they were meant always to be external to the man and subservient to him. In the deep heart of the man was a shrine where none but God was worthy to come. Within him was God; without, a thousand gifts which God had showered upon him. But sin has introduced complications and has made those very gifts of God a potential source of ruin to the soul. Our woes began when God was forced out of His central shrine and things were allowed to enter. . . . There is within the human heart a tough, fibrous root of fallen life whose nature is to possess, always to possess. It covets things with a deep and fierce passion. . . . The roots of our hearts have grown down into things and we dare not pull up one rootlet lest we die. Things have become necessary to us, a development never originally intended. God's gifts now take the place of God, and the whole course of nature is upset by the monstrous substitution.[1]

So we store for ourselves treasures, securities . . . "things." We are told that the "good life" is about having the home paid off, money in the bank and some extra funds to help us feel secure. These things in and of themselves are not necessarily wrong. But as Dr. Tozer so aptly reminded us, the problem begins when we place our hope and future security in those monetary assets instead of in the Lord God Himself.

Let's remember that Christ is once again holding up the standard of *dependence upon God* which is critical for all church leaders to embrace. Our reliance must be placed solely on the Lord. Many of us may never have lots of money to tempt us in these ways, but it is really an issue of the heart. One does not have to be rich to be caught up in materialism and its false sense of security.

We are instructed to store our treasures in heaven. Just what would those "treasures" be? These are the righteous acts of obedience which are highly valued from God's perspective because they demonstrate our submission to Christ's Lordship. The life that is lived for others and the meeting of their needs is blessed in this way. God says, "You can take that to *My* bank!"

The Master closes this section with a poignant reminder that no one can really serve two bosses at the same time. We must make a choice. Will I place my dependence upon God, or will I trust in the riches of this world? Which one will be my master? Leaders in Christ's church cannot be divided on this issue. We must lead the way by demonstrating the joy of a life devoted to and dependent upon the Savior.

The Cure for Anxiety

Matthew 6 is brought to a close with words of comfort for those who get anxious about how their basic physical needs will be met:

Therefore I tell you, do not worry about your life, what you will eat or drink; or about your body, what you will wear. Is not life more important than food, and the body more important than clothes? Look at the birds of the air; they do not sow or reap or store away in barns, and yet your heavenly Father feeds them. Are you not much more valuable than they? Who of you by worrying can add a single hour to his life? And why do you worry about clothes? See how the lilies of the field grow. They do not labor or spin. Yet I tell you that not even Solomon in all his splendor was dressed like one of these. If that is how God clothes the grass of the field, which is here today and tomorrow is thrown into the fire, will he not much more clothe you, O you of little faith? So do not worry, saying, "What shall we eat?" or "What shall we drink?" or "What shall we wear?" For the pagans run after all these things, and your heavenly Father knows that you need them. But seek first his kingdom and his righteousness, and all these things will be given to you as well. Therefore do not worry about tomorrow, for tomorrow will worry about itself. Each day has enough trouble of its own. (Matthew 6:25-34)

What blessed assurance! As we hunger and thirst after righteousness, God will take care of the details! We can literally kiss our anxieties good-bye! We can depend on the Lord. He is aware of every need—both great and small. And He has promised to provide for each one.

This passage also contains a lovely description of God's fatherly care for us. Jesus refers to the "pagans" as those who have just cause for concern. Because they have rejected Jehovah, they have no guarantee that their basic needs will be met. But those of us who have trusted in Christ have the Creator of the Universe as our guarantor. Our Heavenly Father can be counted on in every way.

The matter of a leader's dependence upon God has been brought to the place where the rubber meets the road. As His children who are committed to walking in righteousness, we submit to the Lord and accept everything He brings into our lives—even our needs. Then He will take care of each one.

Leaders in the church need to model this great truth. Though we may not struggle for the basic necessities (food, clothing, shelter) as some of our dear brothers and sisters in other parts of the world, we can still demonstrate our dependence upon the Lord in other tangible ways. Those who are watching us need to see our commitment to this principle: when we seek the kingdom of God and His righteousness, He will take care of the rest!

It is important to note that Christ took twenty verses to talk about the relationship between material things and hungering for His righteousness. Things haven't changed much from His time to ours. Human nature continues the intense struggle between greediness and Godliness. So much value is placed on the possession of material things in our culture.

Believers should stand out in the crowd on this issue. It should be plain for all to see that we refuse to bow down to the false gods of money and things. This should be apparent first and foremost among the leaders of any given congregation. Their hot pursuit of holiness will enable them to say no to the sin of avarice.

Just think of the decisions that would be impacted by embracing Matthew 6:25-34. It might affect the kind of car we drive. This could make a difference when it comes to the size of the home we purchase. It ought to impact the kind and number of "toys" we buy. In the light of the vast needs of people locally, nationally and internationally, Godly leaders need to give consideration to the example they are setting by the things they do or do not purchase. A friend of mine puts the challenge this way: Have we been called to live like *a king*, or is God asking us to live like *the King*?

Blessed are the humble.
Blessed are the broken.
Blessed are the submissive.
Blessed are the dependent.
Not one of the disciples could have guessed that these would be the principles around which the kingdom of Christ would be built. And if we had

lived during the time of Christ, we would have been shocked, too. But stay tuned. There are more surprises to come.

⚑ LEADERSHIP REFLECTIONS

1. How do your leaders demonstrate their dependence in having accountable relationships not only to God but also with one another?
2. How does a personal hunger for God impact our leadership relationships? Where do we see Jesus modeling this principle?

MERCY

THE LORD'S GREAT MERCY freely given to the church leader enables him to have a better understanding of God, and empowers him to be merciful toward those he is leading.

FIVE

Merciful Heavens!

Blessed are the merciful,
for they will be shown mercy.
(Matthew 5:7)

*I*n *The Merchant of Venice*, William Shake-speare penned these famous words:

The quality of mercy is not strained. It droppeth as the gentle rain from heaven upon the place beneath. It is twice blest: it blesseth him that gives it and him that receives. It is the mightiest in the mighty; it becomes the throne of the monarch better than the crown.[1]

The bard had good reason to be so ebullient in his description of the blessings and benefits of mercy. We seem to particularly love this character quality when we are the recipients! But Christ teaches in Matthew 5 that His leaders need to show the way when it comes to offering mercy.

Mercy Defined

Webster defines mercy as "a blessing that is an act of divine favor or compassion; imprisonment rather than death imposed as a penalty. Mercy implies compassion that forebears punishing even when justice demands it."

The Greek word for mercy used in this text is *eleaymonos*. It means simply this: to aid the afflicted, to help the wretched, to rescue the miserable. In biblical usage, "mercy" goes in two directions: first, a kindness shown to someone in need; second, a punishment withheld from a guilty person. When we forgive, pardon or "let someone off the hook," we have extended mercy to that person.

Obviously, the greatest example of mercy in human history is the way in which God has dealt with us through the work of His Son. Though His utter holiness and justice would demand that people be punished for their sins, our heavenly Father sent His only Son to take all of our iniquities upon Himself so that we could experience His marvelous mercy and grace.

A man and his son were forced to walk along a highway one afternoon when their car ran out of gas. As large trucks went rushing by, dark shadows passed over them and the wind whipped their backs. The little child trembled as he clutched his father tightly. When they were safe at home that evening, the boy told his mother about the scary walk they had taken. The father said, "Son, we can be thankful that we were only hit by the shadow of those trucks, and not the trucks themselves!"

Jesus Christ was hit by the full force of the "truck" of His Father's wrath against sin. Only the shadow of God's fury passed over us. In the words of Isaiah: "But he was pierced for our transgressions, he was crushed for our iniquities; the punishment that brought us peace was upon him, and by his wounds we are healed" (Isaiah 53:5).

Chuck Colson visited a prison near the city of Sao Jose dos Campos, Brazil. The government had turned the operation of this facility over to two Christians some twenty years earlier. The institution was renamed Humaita. For two decades, it has been managed according to Christian principles. Mr. Colson tells of his visit to Humaita. The inmates were smiling. The men were at peace.

The guide escorted him to a notorious section of the prison that was once used for torture. Now, that block only housed one prisoner. Colson says:

> As we reached the end of a long concrete corridor and he put the key in the lock, he paused and asked, "Are you sure you want to go in?"
>
> "Of course," I replied. "I've been in isolation cells all over the world."
>
> Slowly he swung open the massive door, and I saw the prisoner in that punishment cell: a crucifix, beautifully carved by the Humaita inmates—the prisoner Jesus, hanging on a cross. "He's doing time for the rest of us," my guide said softly.[2]

Mercy and Christlikeness

God's call to leaders is that we would respond to such love and grace by becoming conduits of His mercy to others. Being recipients of the Father's compassion gives us a new perspective on other people. We develop a fresh desire to offer grace and forgiveness to our fellow sinners. In this way, *being* Christlike will lead to *doing* what the Savior would do. In the words of D. Martyn Lloyd-Jones:

> The Christian gospel places all its primary emphasis upon being, rather than doing. The gospel puts a greater weight upon our attitude than upon our actions. . . . A Christian is something before he does anything. . . . To be Christian is to possess a certain character and therefore to be a certain type of person. . . . We are not meant to control our Christlikeness; our Christlikeness is rather meant to control us.[3]

In this way, *acts* of mercy come from the *facts* celebrated by the Apostle Paul in Galatians 2: "I have been crucified with Christ and I no longer live, but Christ lives in me. The life I live in the body, I live by faith in the Son of God, who loved me and gave himself for me" (Galatians 2:20).

Mercy in the life of the church leader is based on this blessed awareness: Just as God deals with sin on the basis of grace, He deals with the results of sin on the grounds of mercy. Knowing this will protect us from making a major mistake in our ministry to people. As evangelicals, we are concerned with the souls of others—and rightly so. But sometimes we ignore the practical ways in which sin has wounded that soul. For instance, there are times when iniquity leads to poverty. Such folks would be more likely to hear the gospel on a full stomach.

Sadly, pastors or other church leaders who want to move in this direction are often labeled "liberal," or referred to as those who preach "a social gospel." But the evidence is clear that Christ ministered to the whole person—physically, mentally and emotionally as well as spiritually. He fed and healed those who came to Him with these needs.

The story is told of a seminary professor who wanted his students to grasp what it really means to be merciful. So he gave them an assignment on the subject of mercy that required a large amount of research. In order to complete the task, the entire class had to go to the library on the same evening and finish the paper that same night.

On the steps leading to the library, the professor had placed an elderly gentlemen who looked as though he had been injured in a fall. He was unable to help himself. Of the twenty students in the class, only two even stopped to look at the wounded man. Only one actually provided assistance, but this made it impossible for him to get the paper done.

The next day, the seminary prof drove his point home. While the vast majority hurried by in order to get their paper on mercy finished on time, just one actually took the time to *be* merciful! While the others were writing about it, he was practicing it. Needless to say, the student who showed mercy not only passed the teacher's exam—he passed God's test, too.

The subtle message in our culture is that caring for the needy is someone else's job. "There must be some government program to assist them," we say, as we get caught up in reaching goals and developing programs. Like the seminary students, we can be content to theorize about Christlikeness without actually demonstrating it. But God wants to use His church to demonstrate His grace and mercy in the everyday lives of hurting people.

The body of Christ needs to experience a new understanding of God's mercy and all of its implications. It's not just about helping people with the issues of sin. We are also called to minister to those dreadful circumstances that result from multiple transgressions—regardless of whether the victim of the transgression is also the transgressor. Thank God for many evangelical congregations who are targeting unwed mothers, homosexuals, single parents, the indigent and others who are experiencing the ravages of personal and cultural unrighteousness.

Our Messiah came as Healer and Helper as well as Savior and Lord. Leaders need to be reminded of what Christ said when He unrolled the scroll in the synagogue:

> The Spirit of the Lord is on me,
> because he has anointed me
> to preach good news to the poor.
> He has sent me to proclaim freedom
> for the prisoners
> and recovery of sight for the blind,
> to release the oppressed,
> to proclaim the year of the Lord's
> favor. (Luke 4:18-19)

Certainly, this text refers to those who are poor in spirit, held captive by sin, blinded by their own iniquity, and downtrodden by Satan in a spiritual sense. But it must also be interpreted literally. The life and ministry of Jesus corroborate this fact. He also meant those who were *physically* poor, imprisoned, blind and oppressed.

How grateful we can be that the Savior always works with the complete person. We, too, must conduct our ministries in the same manner. Though some will just use Jesus for physical or emotional blessings and reject His salvation, we must continue to offer the whole Christ for the whole person.

Can all of this be taken too far? Is it possible to fall into the trap of poor theology while developing a theology of the poor? Could we become so focused on the down-and-outers that we neglect the up-and-outers, a.k.a. "the happy pagans"? All of these dangers are real. But the bottom line is this: church leaders are called by our Lord Jesus to demonstrate God's mercy in practical ways. This is the essence of Christlikeness.

So it must be stated that it is not acceptable to take the gospel alone to those in need. It's a classic case of "show and tell." We must *show* His mercy first before we can *tell* them about it. We assist the indigent with their immediate needs for food, clothing, and shelter. We change the oil in the car of a busy single mother who lacks the time and money to do it herself. We help the elderly person who needs a ride to church or the grocery store. We pay the bills of the unemployed. We listen to the lonely. We play golf with the country-clubbers, attend dinner meetings of the local chamber of commerce and pray with and for business and community leaders.

Being merciful is being able to see through the eyes of a spiritually impoverished person. It is hearing the obscenities that an abused wife has heard. It is knowing the pain of losing a job. And as we put ourselves in their place, we will be anointed to offer a plan of action to help these dear ones. Leaders who allow themselves to empathize with those who are hurting will truly be able to serve the church and the world for Christ.

Mercy Is Risky Business

Most of us—perhaps all of us—agree that mercy is a great thing, and we should be more generous with it. We all know how good it feels to be on the receiving end of compassion—so why do we not practice it on a more regular basis? One reason may be that it entails a certain element of danger. David Johnson points out that showing mercy was risky business in our Lord's day as well as in our time:

> Some people see the practice of mercy as a sign of weakness. The Romans were merciless, and that kind of coldness was a highly valued virtue in that era. They thought that mercy was something that weakened people. It kept one from doing the hard thing and making the difficult decisions. Stoics referred to mercy as a "disease of the soul." Why? Because it makes you soft and indecisive. . . . If you are a merciful person, there's

a high probability that you'll get run over.
We hear stories about those who tried to be
the Good Samaritan, and rather than being
rewarded, they were robbed, raped, or ran-
sacked. And they end up saying things like
this: "I won't be tricked into showing compassion ever again! I was a fool to be merciful. . . . Out there in the real world where
things are rough and tough, it's just a 'no
mercy' society."[4]

Many pastors and church leaders know that they
should demonstrate this Christlike quality of mercy,
but they, too, are afraid that they will get hammered!
No one wants to get burned. Many of us have been
conned by people who convinced us that they had a
serious financial need. After assistance was given, the
scam was uncovered. The temptation is to say,
"Well, I just can't help *anyone* because you never
know who really needs it and who's just a fraud!"

It is true that we live in a day when discernment is
absolutely necessary to distinguish between the genuine and the false. But even if we do get "taken for a
ride" from time to time, we must never give up.
Showing mercy is required of all church leaders—not
just those who have never been swindled. All of us are
to display compassion regardless of the risks.

Merciful Hindrances

In Matthew 7, the Savior points out several hindrances to being merciful. His purpose here is to
bring this character trait into the real world. Christ

deals with judging one another, discernment and the true meaning of giving.

First, He underlines the importance of mercy in His warning against a judgmental attitude:

> Do not judge, or you too will be judged. For in the same way you judge others, you will be judged, and with the measure you use, it will be measured to you.
>
> Why do you look at the speck of sawdust in your brother's eye and pay no attention to the plank in you own eye? How can you say to your brother, "Let me take the speck out of your eye," when all the time there is a plank in your own eye? You hypocrite, first take the plank out of your own eye, and then you will see clearly to remove the speck from your brother's eye. (Matthew 7:1-5)

Jesus is saying, "Here's the deal: unless your life is absolutely perfect, don't set yourself up as a judge of everyone else." He has touched upon the foremost tool of Satan for the destruction of the church. Judgmental folks have blinded and destroyed many members of Christ's body by poking their eyes with constant criticism. Our daily prayer should be, "Lord, help me clean up my own act, and give me the grace to allow *You* to work on others without interference from me."

Are there times when church leaders need to "judge" and "discipline" straying believers? Absolutely. But the best preparation for this is to deal with our own sin. As we judge ourselves, our hearts remain tender toward those who have fallen.

A critical spirit was a very real problem with the scribes and Pharisees. Their laws favored compliance with external rules instead of developing internal character. This made it much easier to assess others. With clipboard and checklist in hand, they could observe those around them and make snap judgments about their holiness or lack thereof.

These misguided spiritual guides of the Jews were also very good at putting on an act of outward holiness. They knew precisely when it was "show time." They quickly figured out how to pass each other's tests so that they were free to focus on the weaknesses of those who were not quite there yet.

Unfortunately, the Jewish people copied what they saw in their leaders. They were quick to criticize the slightest misstep, often basing their judgments on rumor and innuendo instead of facts. The rule books were thick and the tension in the air was thicker.

This same dilemma plagues the church today. So many want to set themselves up as everyone's judge, with an unwritten rule book of outward behavior. A pastor friend of mine shared the story of a man and woman who came to Christ while they were living together. They came under conviction for this arrangement and wanted to get married. The pastor suggested that they refrain from sexual relations and live in separate apartments for the two months prior to their marriage, and the couple agreed.

He told his elders about these wonderful conversions. The couple was willing to live apart for two months. The leaders were thrilled until the pastor asked if they could use the church for the wedding. A few "holier than thou" judges slammed their gavels and said, "No! Not in my church!" So the pastor performed a lovely outdoor wedding ceremony in a nearby park.

How sad! Two people are transformed by the saving power of Christ. Their sins are forgiven, and they give proof of the sincerity of their repentance by living separately for two months. And even though God was certainly pleased and more than willing to accept them into His house, this man and woman were not good enough for a few of those elders.

To immature leaders such as these, Christ issues this warning in Matthew 7:2: "For in the same way you judge others, you will be judged, and with the measure you use, it will be measured to you." We are so quick to judge others. For example, if a church leader were seen walking out of a bar with a smile on his face, many parishioners would think, *I didn't know he had a drinking problem!* But he may have been smiling because he had just shared the gospel with a lost and lonely soul in that place.

One issue in which many believers act as judge and jury is divorce. Without knowing the facts, it is easy to make assumptions about someone whose marriage fails. The church has plenty of rules around this issue to ensure the "purity" of our leaders. But in the process, many wonderful believers have been left out.

I remember the agony of dealing with a couple in this category. They were so excited in their newfound faith in Christ. As they were discipled, they became aware of the urgent needs overseas and committed themselves to pursuing a missionary career.

Unfortunately, their application was summarily rejected by several denominations and parachurch organizations because the wife had been divorced and remarried. The circumstances of her failed marriage were well known to me and should have been taken into consideration. She had been married while still a teenager—just out of high school. Neither she nor her husband were Christians at that time. Shortly after the wedding, her husband went into the military and was later transferred overseas, which separated the couple for many months at a time. He became involved with other women and decided to leave her. Though she tried her best to reconcile the marriage, he was determined to divorce her; she had no other alternative.

Years later, she met her present husband; they were both led to Christ by the chaplain who performed their wedding. They had a passion to serve the Lord, but few mission agencies would consider them because of something that happened years before either of them was born again.

Was it merciful to judge this couple in the present based on the past? Does it not make more sense to look at them through Christ's eyes as those who are completely forgiven? Doesn't Paul's statement in Second Corinthians carry some weight here? "Therefore, if anyone is in Christ, he is a new creation; the old has gone, the new has come!" (2 Corinthians 5:17).

This is a critical issue with which denominational leaders, pastors and local church leaders must grapple. Will we take the easy way out by falling back on our rule books and formulas, or will we seek to show mercy even as God has poured His mercy upon us? Good and godly leaders will honestly disagree on this kind of issue. But if we err, why not err on the side of mercy?

It is amazing to watch the reaction of Christians who find out that some people in the body of Christ used to be homosexuals, supporters of abortion or prostitutes. We tend to reject these folks on the basis of what they *used to be*. But this is diametrically opposed to God's response of grace and love!

And what about those who are *still* outside of Christ but desperately need to hear of the Redeemer's plan of salvation? Will we offer them mercy or judgment? It is so easy to get caught up in trying to fix the world's sin that we can reject the sinner whom Christ loves. It is dangerous to assume that they don't want to hear the gospel. Remember Peter's statement about God's patience? "He is patient with you, not wanting anyone to perish, but everyone to come to repentance" (2 Peter 3:9).

No Mercy

Our Lord balances His teaching on showing mercy by citing the danger of tolerating sin and rejection in the name of compassion: "Do not give dogs what is sacred; do not throw your pearls to pigs. If you do, they may trample them under their feet, and then turn and tear you to pieces" (Matthew 7:6).

There is always perfect balance in the righteousness of God. It is possible to get so carried away with the propagation of mercy that we may even waste our time by offering it to those who are chronically antagonistic to the Savior's love. Jesus refers to those who continually reject the truth as "pigs." Pigs were ceremonially unclean, so the Jews could relate to this as a symbol of the lowest form of carnality. In essence, Christ is saying that those hardened adversaries have sacrificed their right to His Father's mercy and grace.

I remember seeing a television newscast which profiled a street preacher who was shouting over a loud speaker at a young lady who was a prostitute. This lady of the night was attempting to solicit support for the legalization of prostitution in New York City. The minister was screaming at her relentlessly, "You need to get saved! Give up your sin! You're going to hell!"

This young man probably thought he was doing the kingdom of God a big favor by bellowing the so-called "good news" at this call girl. It was quite obvious, however, that she was not the least bit interested in what he had to say. And she was particularly annoyed by the manner in which he was saying it. Most of the passers-by would ordinarily have ignored her, but thanks to the street preacher she had their sympathy—and the preacher had their scorn.

Is this not a modern-day version of "giving pearls to pigs"? The hooker at first ignored and eventually attacked the street preacher—with the support of the crowd. It may be difficult to accept, but some people have made up their mind never to bow their knee to Lordship of Jesus Christ. The Savior says, "Love them, but leave them alone." "Truth" pearls are too valuable to waste.

Instead, we are to move on to those who are more receptive. As the Master sent out the Twelve on their first mission, He told them, "If anyone will not welcome you or listen to your words, shake the dust off your feet when you leave that home or town" (Matthew 10:14).

Discernment is a vital necessity for the church leader. There are times when our merciful acts are wasted on "pigs." A young man in the Corinthian church was involved with his father's wife (1 Corinthians 5:1) and had apparently rejected the loving and merciful urgings of the church leaders to leave this sinful lifestyle. Paul said that the next step was to withdraw the first kind of mercy and institute another kind of compassion—caring enough to discipline the sinner. No more lectures; he wasn't listening anyway. The church was told to excommunicate this rebellious person (5:2-5). It was the flip side of the mercy coin. Today, we call this "tough love."

The thrilling conclusion of the story, recorded in Second Corinthians 2, is that the young man seems to have eventually repented of his immorality and came back to Christ. His change of heart was such a shock to the leaders in Corinth that they didn't know quite how to handle him. Paul said, "Now instead, you ought to forgive and comfort him, so that he will not be overwhelmed by excessive sorrow. I urge you, therefore, to reaffirm your love for him" (2 Corinthians 2:7-8).

Genuine Mercy

Our Lord sums up His teaching on mercy with these words:

> Ask and it will be given to you; seek and you will find; knock and the door will be opened to you. For everyone who asks receives; he who seeks finds; and to him who knocks, the door will be opened.
>
> Which of you, if his son asks for bread, will give him a stone? Or if he asks for a fish, will give him a snake? If you, then, though you are evil, know how to give good gifts to your children, how much more will your Father in heaven give good gifts to those who ask him! So in everything, do to others what you would have them do to you, for this sums up the Law and the Prophets. (Matthew 7:7-12)

If someone comes to us and says, "I am hungry," the temptation is to give them something to eat, but nothing more. Is that all that is required of us as servants of the Lord? Jesus reminds us here that we need to be sensitive to giving *beyond* what is being asked. Felt needs are not always real needs. He illustrates this with an example from His Father's generosity. When we want "good gifts," He offers the best—His Holy Spirit.

When we first become believers, we may not be very knowledgeable about Christianity. We are quite satisfied just to have our sins forgiven. Many Christians continue at that level for the rest of their lives—grateful to be forgiven and on the way to heaven. It seems to end right there.

But is this really the full extent of God's gift to us in salvation? Indeed, God gives us new life, but it is also *abundant* life! He has given us His Spirit to comfort, convict, guide and direct. The same Holy Spirit also blesses us with His gifts for service. There is so much more than merely being forgiven and heaven-bound!

We are to give in like manner as we have received. In a word—*abundantly*! When someone comes to us with a need, we should help them with the immediate problem as an act of mercy. But we must take the next step. Are there underlying issues that created the need?

If a man asks for $50 to buy groceries for his family, it is easy enough for the church to write a check from the benevolent fund and send him on his way. But have we really helped him? Have we really demonstrated mercy God's way? Should we not find out if he is unemployed? And if that is the case, are we not obligated to do our best to find him a suitable job?

After a little digging, we may discover that this man has not been able to hold down a job because of a struggle with alcohol—and we have a Savior who can deliver him from his addiction. A simple request for grocery money becomes an opportunity to meet an individual's social, emotional, physical and spiritual needs in the name of Christ. That is "giving the good gift," acting from a heart made truly merciful by the transforming power of God's Spirit. The merciful leader looks beyond the obvious and in Christ's power discerns the real need.

Genuine mercy is a heart attitude of compassion for people—meeting people where they are with what they need. In ministering on this level, we can show them that their greatest need is total dependence upon God. This will move them to a new level in their relationship with Christ and provide the foundation on which they can cope with every circumstance of life.

This leadership principle is transforming for the giver as well as the receiver. Most leaders are so task-oriented that the needs of real people can get lost in the shuffle. And although we can and should be motivated by the mission to which we are called, leaders who are true servants of Christ must balance a drive to get things done with a genuine love for others.

Matthew 5:7 was the original call for the church to be "seeker sensitive." But the Master took this principle much further than is implied by congregations who claim this label. He was not just talking about being in tune with their way of thinking. Jesus wants us to be sensitive to the whole seeker. We are to show mercy for the full range of human need.

As the Savior began multiplying leaders throughout His three-year ministry, He could see how important humility, brokenness, meekness, dependence
and mercy would be in carrying out this enormous
task of building His church. "Making disciples of all
nations" was a tall order; it could only happen
through those men and women who had realized just
how much they needed Him.

Now the Lord of the Church adds another indis-
pensable item: holiness.

✈ LEADERSHIP REFLECTIONS

1. Mercy requires us to put people first in a very
   task-oriented culture. How does Jesus expect us
   to live this character quality in our church leadership?
2. Find two or three passages that show Jesus acting
   this way. What are the implications for how we
   do church?

HOLINESS

THE CHURCH LEADER IS motivated by the singular desire to live a pure and holy life by intimately knowing God and seeing Him in every situation.

CHAPTER
SIX

Wholly Holy

Blessed are the pure in heart,
for they will see God.

(Matthew 5:8)

Who does not want to see and know God? But do we really? Are we willing to pay the price required to apprehend God's purity and beauty? Whatever the cost, it is well worth it. Gary Thomas says, "Grasping the beauty of God is key to holiness and discernment. . . . Spiritual beauty creates the context for our obedience, and it serves to refine our spiritual taste so that valuing what God values, seeing things His way, becomes a passion and joy."[1]

Even though it seems difficult to attain and maintain, it makes sense that purity is an essential trait of leaders in the kingdom of God. Why? Because those who lead the flock must have vision. And that vision is the result of pure passion and motivation so fixed in the Lord's righteousness that all other dreams and plans become secondary.

George Barna defines *vision* as that which is "a clear mental image of a preferable future imparted by God to His chosen servants and is based upon an accurate understanding of God, self, and circumstances."[2]

Notice the fascinating statement by Jesus at the end of Matthew 5:8: "For they will see God." This "clear mental image" will only come to those with a pure heart. The leader whose life is committed in this direction will "see God" in every circumstance of life. A holy heart will enable leaders to have an unclouded vision. And as we see God we can know what He is saying and doing, so that we can become a part of His work right where we serve.

Pure in Heart

Purity of heart is an *internal* issue. The Greek word for *heart* is often used in conjunction with internal realities. It pertains to the seat of our personality, the inner person—or as we say, "The real you and me." One commentator clarifies this for us:

> The heart denotes the seat of intellectual and spiritual life, the inner life in opposition to external appearance. The heart stands for man's ego. It is simply the person ("the hidden person of the heart . . ." [1 Peter 3:4]). The heart is that in man which is addressed by God. It is the seat of doubt and hardness as well as of faith and obedience. . . . It is the person, the thinking, feeling, willing ego of man, with particular regard to his responsibility to God, that the New Testament denotes by the use of heart.[3]

It should also be noted that the word for *heart* and the word for *mind* are used closely together in many texts. But when either word is used by itself, there is a more distinct meaning attached to it. *Mind* is used in cases where the element of knowledge is more prominent. *Heart* is employed for those times when the writers wanted to emphasize the aspects of emotion and will.

Some would try to make the mind and heart synonymous. But this could lead to a number of wrong conclusions about God's dealings with mankind. We need to understand that the heart is a reference to our inner being. Everything that we are flows from this area. It includes the mind, the feelings and the will, yet it is not limited to those three. God always speaks to the heart because it is the seat of faith.

God is chiefly concerned that we have pure hearts based on an inner change, the direct result of the work of His Spirit in our lives. It is not simply through the mind or the emotions that our Lord captures us. His Word pierces our very being. We can know about God with our minds on an intellectual level. We can also experience Him to an extent through our emotions. But no salvation or transformation can take place apart from that supernatural invasion by the Spirit into the human heart.

Seeing God

When my wife and I were attending Bible college many years ago, we had some close friends in that school who were newlyweds, living in a tiny basement apartment. They literally made it through college on prayer. They had no money. The parents on both sides were not Christians, and they were not supportive of the faith journey their children had chosen.

There were many days when they had little or no food in the house. On one particular day when the refrigerator was totally empty, they prayed that God would somehow provide food for them. As they were praying, the wife's mother arrived unexpectedly with several bags of groceries. The couple began to weep as they praised the Lord for answering their petition.

But the mother looked at her daughter and said very sternly, "Don't thank God—thank me! After all, I'm the one who brought the food to you!"

The daughter looked her mother right in the eye and said, "God can even use those who do not belong to Him to do His will." She was not condemning her mom; she simply wanted her mother to see the Lord, who had promised to meet their needs. Because of their purity of heart and simple faith, they witnessed the presence of Christ in the midst of desperate circumstances.

Since that time, this woman's mother became a lovely Christian, too. She is now able to see God—even in difficult circumstances. And though the Lord had used her to answer prayer even before she knew Him as Savior, only the pure in heart were actually able to see it.

Capturing the true vision of God is like walking out into the night sky and being able to see it through the eyes of an astronomer. The average person can only observe what appears to be an infinite number of stars in no particular order. But the trained scientist can note each constellation in its unique position in the sky. The astronomer has a relationship with the stars that most of us could not understand.

Another way to think of "blessed are the pure in heart, for they will *see* God" comes from the world of art. When I walk into an art gallery, I can become easily distracted, even bored. My taste goes in the opposite direction of what most consider to be "art" today. I prefer paintings of barns, silos and windmills—realistic things. But a real artist can stare for long periods of time at what I would call "blobs of paint." He may even have an elevated heartbeat looking at things that put me to sleep. Why? He has a relationship with art that I simply do not have.

In a similar way, those who are pure in heart have a relationship with God that allows them to observe the Lord in ways that an impure person cannot. This is the meaning of Jesus' words. The world is easily confused by watching Christians who say "Praise the Lord" even when circumstances are dark and dreary.

The notion that believers actually *want* to spend a Sunday morning worshiping, praying and listening to a sermon is inexplicable to the unbeliever. To them, it appears to be a waste of time. They just don't get it. However, we should not expect them to be interested because of what Christ said in Matthew 5:8. Only those who have hearts purified by the Lord Jesus can know what it means to know and see God the Father.

The Undivided Heart

Asa was one of the better kings of Judah, but the final years of his reign were marred by continual war because, in a moment of crisis, he sought help from the king of Syria instead of trusting the Lord his God. In announcing God's judgment, Hanani the seer voiced the truth that Asa had apparently forgotten: "for the eyes of the LORD range throughout the earth in order to strengthen those whose hearts are fully committed to him" (2 Chronicles 16:9). Jehovah is always looking for those who will place their entire confidence in Him alone. This is another way of saying that God wants those with a pure, undivided heart.

He is primarily concerned with our hearts and our inner relationship with Him. The Lord knows that a leader whose heart is divided will struggle to give godly guidance to the church. Blessed are the pure in heart—those who have focused in on God like a laser beam. No turning back. No fading to the right or the left. These servants are intensely concentrated on seeing the Lord in all His glory.

The Passions of a Pure Heart

Northern Europe and Asia are home to the ermine, a mink-like animal which is highly valued for its snowy white fur. The ermine is obsessed with keeping its white coat absolutely spotless and pure. Unfortunately, such fastidiousness often leads to its capture.

Those hunting the ermine start by finding its den in a rock pile or the hollow of a tree. While the animal is away from its hideout, the poachers put filth all over the opening. The ermine naturally goes home when being pursued, but on finding that its home is a mess, it refuses to enter and becomes an easy prey.

How wonderful it would be to have a church full of people who were as fanatical about internal purity as the ermine is about external purity! While a passion for cleanliness can cost the ermine its life, a deep passion for holiness can be the key to abundant life for us, for "without holiness no one will see the Lord" (Hebrews 12:14). An understanding of this can be found in Psalm 51, which begins with this confession:

> Have mercy on me, O God,
>   according to your unfailing love;
> according to your great compassion
>   blot out my transgressions.
> Wash away all my iniquity
>   and cleanse me from my sin.
>
> For I know my transgressions,
>   and my sin is always before me.
>   (51:1-3)

King David was acutely aware of his utter sinfulness in this confession of his adultery with Bathsheba and the subsequent murder of her husband. If he had been using Jesus' words, he might have said, "I am poor in spirit—I am mourning because of my iniquity." David submits himself to

God's judgment for his sin to demonstrate his brokenness before the Lord:

> Against you, you only, have I sinned
> and done what is evil in your sight,
> so that you are proved right when you
> speak
> and justified when you judge. (51:4)

David realized the impending doom of an impure heart. Sin had separated him from God's holy presence. He was unable to experience His fellowship and power. The joy was gone, along with his ability to share the love of Jehovah with anyone else. But his passion for a pure heart longed for the cleansing of God's forgiveness:

> Hide your face from my sins
> and blot out my iniquity.
>
> Create in me a pure heart, O God,
> and renew a steadfast spirit within
> me.
> Do not cast me from your presence
> or take your Holy Spirit from me.
> Restore to me the joy of your salvation
> and grant me a willing spirit, to
> sustain me.
> Then I will teach transgressors your
> ways,
> and sinners will turn back to you.
> (51:9-13)

David also wanted to get back into a relationship with Jehovah that was in line with the first and greatest commandment. He wanted to once again love the Lord with all his heart, soul and mind. King David wanted to return to that union with God that was characterized by complete obedience and dependence:

> Surely you desire truth in the inner
>> parts;
>> you teach me wisdom in the inmost
>>> place . . . .
> The sacrifices of God are a broken
>> spirit;
>> a broken and contrite heart,
>> O God, you will not despise.
>>> (51:6, 17)

Blessed are those leaders, who, like David, commit themselves utterly to the pursuit of God and a pure heart.

Impure Purity

Jesus dealt with the subject of a pure heart repeatedly when He addressed the Pharisees, because they were so concerned with externals. Instead of searching for the real meaning of God's truth, these blind leaders were content to play games with the letter of the law. When the Pharisees complained that Christ's disciples were not following all their elaborate rules, the Master responded,

> Woe to you, teachers of the law and Pharisees, you hypocrites! You are like whitewashed tombs, which look beautiful on the outside but on the inside are full of dead

> men's bones and everything unclean. In the
> same way, on the outside you appear to
> people as righteous but on the inside you
> are full of hypocrisy and wickedness. (Mat-
> thew 23:27-28)

Pay a visit to a cemetery: the grass is green and
well-trimmed; the shrubs are artistically sculptured;
colorful flowers are planted among the graves. It's a
wonderful place for a stroll. Yet in reality a cemetery
is just an elaborate cover-up. Underneath the beauti-
ful sod and floral bouquets are rows of coffins, decaying flesh and deteriorating bones.

Jesus was telling the Pharisees that their lives
were also an elaborate coverup. Though on the outside they looked pure and clean, their inner hearts
were impure and their motives self-seeking. In that
sense, it was an "impure purity." But Christ calls
His people and their leaders to a life that is pure
from the inside out. In fact, our Master tells us, outward behavior is meaningless apart from inward holiness.

When the nation of Israel selected their first
king, it was little more than a "beauty contest."
Saul was the most impressive candidate because of
his physical stature. It is a myth of leadership that
the biggest and strongest, the tallest and best looking are the best leaders. (I heard recently that someone was nominated for the presidency of an
organization primarily because he "looked presi-
dential"!)

Superior leadership, however, has nothing to do with the ability to run the farthest, jump the highest or throw the ball the farthest. This is probably why God took over the voting booth for Israel's second king. He chose a shepherd boy, the youngest in his family—the runt of the litter! But David was selected because of his undivided heart for God.

All of us can get caught up in judging others on the basis of externals, just like the Pharisees. Many churches have a "rule book" of their own, with membership contingent upon signing a "lifestyle statement"—a commitment not to smoke, drink, use illegal drugs, etc. It is a modern attempt to legislate holiness by decree, just like the religious leaders of our Lord's day.

But it didn't work for the Pharisees and it won't work today. The only thing that can come from man-made holiness is an impure imitation of the real thing. The leaders of the flock of Christ need to have pure hearts based on the verses preceding Matthew 5:8. Because they are humbled, broken, gentle, dependent and merciful (Matthew 5:3-7), they can embrace genuine holiness.

Holiness as a Way of Life

Christ once again brings all of this teaching home to where we live. Those listening were familiar with the narrow gates and passageways around Jerusalem. To illustrate the matter of a pure, holy heart, the Savior takes this everyday experience and gives it spiritual significance: "Enter through the narrow gate. For wide is the gate and broad is the road that leads to destruction, and many enter through it. But small is the gate and narrow the road that leads to life, and only a few find it" (Matthew 7:13-14).

It is a narrow gate, leading to a narrow way. Only a few will find this way to holiness of heart and eternal life. Modern Christianity would try to persuade us otherwise. The way is simple and broad, some would have us believe; we can live for Christ without really giving anything up. Perhaps we should rewrite the story of the rich young man in Matthew 19. The modern version would have Jesus instructing this wealthy young executive to accept Him and then "be a witness" to his materialistic, upperclass friends. No change would be necessary; the affluent young man would not need to forsake any aspect of his opulent lifestyle.

But the biblical narrative is quite clear. Christ could read the mind and heart of this man. His god was money. Though he might be able to believe in the Messiah on a shallow, intellectual level, he was unable to give his *heart* to the Lord. The apartment on Fifth Avenue and the Porsche had to go if he was to make a commitment to Christ. Vast wealth may not be a problem for everyone, but it certainly was for this man.

God requires that we come to Him in total dependence with a humble spirit, broken by the reality of our sinfulness. Those who desire to lead Christ's church must come with nothing to offer, no one to protect them, nowhere else to turn. We must not "try" Jesus—instead, we must trust Him with our very lives.

What did the Savior mean when He said, "only a few ever find it"? The extended meaning here is that fewer still choose to *continue* in the way of holiness once they begin. It is a difficult pathway! Our hearts need to be submitted not just for that initial cleansing, but also for the *continual* purification by His Spirit.

The parable of the soils (Mark 4:1-20) addresses this issue. The "good soil" (4:20) represents those who find the narrow way, enter through the blood of Christ, and remain in obedience to Him. The "rocky places" (4:16) and the "thorns" (4:18) describe the fate of those who never really become a part of God's kingdom. They come to the narrow gate, try it for a while and perhaps even commit to some external behaviors. But they never really submit to Christ or the demands of this strenuous commitment. So these folks eventually fall away.

All of this sounds harsh and intolerant because . . . *it is*! God is literally looking for people who are willing to live out "radical" Christianity. He wants us to seek Him with *all* our hearts, souls and minds. He is looking for followers—disciples, not just intellectual believers who take what they can from Christ and combine it with what they have in themselves.

There is no shortcut. There is no easy way to build the kind of character described by Jesus in Matthew 5. It is the work of the Holy Spirit to produce humility, brokenness, meekness, dependence, mercy and purity in our hearts. But we're not through just yet.

⚑ LEADERSHIP REFLECTIONS

1. How are we as leaders modeling passionate, radical *Christ*ianity to those we are responsible to lead?
2. What would be the impact of our lives as leaders if we truly lived out this passionate compassion of Jesus? How might it impact how we do church?

PEACEMAKING

GODLY LEADERS SEEK TO be men and women who understand the peace of God in their own lives and promote peace through biblical reconciliation in the body of Christ.

CHAPTER
Seven

The Peacemakers

Blessed are the peacemakers,
*   for they will be called sons of God.*
                                (Matthew 5:9)

Those who can lead the way in peacemaking are very welcome in our society today. The business world refers to them as "consultants" or "conflict managers." Such people are in great demand because there is so much strife in our culture and in our churches. William Hendriksen points out why this makes Christianity so relevant:

> In a world of peace-breaking, this beatitude shows what a thoroughly relevant, vital and dynamic force Christianity really is. . . . True peacemakers are all those whose leader is the God of peace, who aspire after peace with all men, proclaim the gospel of peace, and pattern their lives after the Prince of Peace.[1]

And yet, the disciples who first heard this call to peacemaking must have been dumbfounded! Don't forget that our Lord's audience was a group of Jews who were quite convinced that He had come to overthrow the Roman government and set up a new order. But instead of a hostile takeover, this Messiah proclaims the virtue of peacemaking!

Webster's Dictionary defines peace as "a state of tranquillity or quiet; a state of security or order." From the secular perspective, we are to conclude that "peace" is therefore determined by the level of serenity in the circumstances or events surrounding us. But this could not possibly be what Christ was talking about. The people He was speaking to were about to face enormous conflict. Some of them would even become martyrs for the faith. Does that sound "peaceful" to you?

Paul sheds some light on the difference between the world's concept of peace and that which is embraced by believers:

> Rejoice in the Lord always. I will say it again: Rejoice! Let your gentleness be evident to all. The Lord is near. Do not be anxious about anything, but in everything, by prayer and petition, with thanksgiving, present your requests to God. And the peace of God, which transcends all understanding, will guard your hearts and your minds in Christ Jesus. (Philippians 4:4-7)

This is a supernatural brand of peace that possesses the children of God. It is the work of the Holy Spirit in response to the simple faith and obedience of the believer. The unbelieving world cannot grasp this truth. It is sometimes difficult even for Christians to so completely trust the Lord that this peace takes over. But the promise is that His peace will guard both the heart (our emotions) and the mind (our thinking). What a powerful promise in a day when medications for depression, loneliness and acid indigestion are big sellers across our country.

Peace with God

The church leader can know the peace *of* God because he or she has peace *with* God. This reconciliation was brought about by the saving work of Jesus Christ. A result of this is that the leader can "always be full of joy in the Lord." He can grow into experiencing a perspective of life that allows him to live above the anxiety which comes about from troubling circumstances.

There is a clear difference here between believers and non-believers. The unsaved person has no source from which to draw strength in the midst of life's trials and tribulations. They may try to look within, or even to friends and loved ones without. But apart from this divine peace, there will only be frustration and despair. They will need peace with God to enjoy the peace of God.

Even many Christians today do not experience the peace of God the way God intended. This is primarily because we tend to be more obsessed with the world than we are with our Lord. We find our meaning and security in the stuff of life; our accumulations of people, positions, money and power become our substitute peace.

The peace of the world is obtained through the strenuous manipulation of circumstances:

"When I have saved enough money, I will be at peace . . ."

"When I can buy that larger home, I will be at peace . . ."

"When I can divorce this spouse and marry that other person, I will be at peace . . ."

Christians, on the other hand, can rest in the Lord because they can see His hand at work in all things. They believe what Paul said in Romans 8: "And we know that in all things God works for the good of those who love him, who have been called according to his purpose" (Romans 8:28).

So many are depressed in our world today. People are popping all kinds of pills to make themselves feel better about life. This is understandable when God is taken out of the equation. After all, we live in a culture that offers much to be despondent about!

As leaders, we must cling to Proverbs 3:5-6: "Trust in the LORD with all your heart and lean not on your own understanding; in all your ways acknowledge him, and he will make your paths straight."

Leaning on our own understanding of our circumstances will only produce trepidation. Completely trusting Christ will yield the peace that can carry us through any difficulty. This trust produces an inner strength that relies on God's provision to help us respond and live in a Christlike manner.

Peace in God

One of the great hindrances to the peace spoken of by Jesus and the Apostle Paul is that we tend to want deliverance *from* trials instead of peace *in the midst of* them. Frequently, the result is that we experience neither. Jerry Bridges challenges us along these lines:

> The result promised to us when we come to God in prayer with thanksgiving is not deliverance, but the peace of God. One of the reasons we don't find this peace is because all too often we will not settle for anything other than deliverance from the trouble. But God, through Paul, promises us peace, a peace that is unexplainable. It transcends all understanding. And, says Paul, it will guard your hearts and minds against the anxiety to which you and I are so prone. . . . Your responsibility is to come in prayer, asking for peace, and looking to him for it.[2]

It is imperative for pastors and church leaders to learn how to "give thanks" *in* every situation—not necessarily *for* every circumstance. This is a subtle but important distinction. If you break your arm in an accident, God does not expect you to say, "Thank you, Lord, *for* this broken arm!" However, you can be at peace and be thankful *in* that situation. You can rest assured that God is in control and that as you respond in a godly manner in the midst of these circumstances you can experience God's peace as He uses you for His purpose.

The Christian young person with an alcoholic father should not be expected to be grateful *for* a dad like that. One would never say, "Lord, I want to thank you for my drunken father." But that same young person can be thankful *in* that situation and can grow spiritually through such an ordeal as he allows the peace of God to rule in his heart.

Job is an illustration of this truth. Here we have a man who was completely dedicated to Jehovah. He avoided evil as if it were a deadly disease, and he sought to please God in every situation. Job was so sensitive about sin that he offered sacrifices after his teenagers had a party to cover any iniquity that may have taken place!

Job was an extremely wealthy man who was living a very comfortable life. The devil accused him of being at peace with God solely because he was enjoying such a charmed life. So in the final verses of chapter 1, Jehovah allows Satan to attack full force. Job is wiped out financially. His family is killed, his servants kidnaped and his flocks and herds stolen. And that was just the first day!

This man of God responded with these memorable words: "Naked I came from my mother's womb, and naked I will depart. The LORD gave and the LORD has taken away; may the name of the LORD be praised" (Job 1:21).

Job knew the peace of God in the midst of prosperity and catastrophe. His tranquility before the Lord was not the result of favorable circumstances—it was the supernatural work of God.

Peace with Others

The leader who is a peacemaker is one who knows the peace of God in the daily circumstances of life.

The serenity of the Holy Spirit has become his life-style. This is the prerequisite for becoming a peace-maker. One definition of those who make peace is that they "reconcile parties who are at a variance."

Of course, the greatest peacemaker of all is the Holy Spirit Himself. He appeased God's wrath through the shed blood of Christ. This results in a peace beyond human comprehension. So then, godly leaders can only mediate the strife in other people's lives when they are at peace with God themselves.

Our Lord has been illustrating this throughout His teaching in Matthew 5-7. The peacemaker must be a person who has been humbled and broken. This is someone who is totally submitted to and dependent upon God. He has a merciful, pure heart. Now he can be involved in bringing reconciliation between man and God as well as peace between feuding men and women.

This is a special word to pastors and church leaders. The Lord wants to give us the ministry of peace-making. It involves introducing people first to their need for repentance and faith in Christ. Then, after leading them to peace with God, they can experience reconciliation with those around them. But mark this: The vertical relationship with God is imperative to the horizontal relationship with others. Paul points this out in Acts 24: "So I strive always to keep my conscience clear before God and man" (24:16).

In fact, all healthy horizontal (people to people) relationships must be first based on one's vertical relationship with God. God has called us as church leaders to lead people into that humble, submitted relationship to God so that they can live out His mercy and peace in human relationships.

A Peace That Motivates

As church leaders we often ask how we can more effectively motivate people to share their faith. We have certainly developed enough training programs and motivational gimmicks. But most of those efforts have failed miserably. Could it be that God is saying something even through our inability to mobilize believers for outreach? I think so.

God's plan begins with the leaders of any given church. They begin to discover that their own motivation for sharing their faith is the peace in their own hearts. As they look around at lost friends, relatives, neighbors and work associates who seem so restless and aimless, they are compelled to share the peace and purpose that comes through a personal relationship with Jesus Christ.

Here again, we see that the Lord works from the inside to the outside. Internal contentment leads to external outreach to those who are struggling.

This is an important facet of effective outreach. There can be no real change of outward behavior without first addressing the inner man. As we uncover the anxious spirit within the unbeliever, he will begin to see his need. But the leader must find and be living his own peace with God in order to bring this blessing to others.

There are many factors which influence the degree to which people will share their faith. Most Christians would say that they are not involved in outreach because they do not know how or because they are too frightened. In response to this, many pastors fire back with blazing sermons on the believer's responsibility to snatch people out of hell. This is usually followed by an invitation to attend an outreach training seminar. But very few people commit. And the whole process looks pathetically like putting a band-aid on a broken arm.

Most people do not share their faith for one simple reason: *They are not excited about what God has done for them!* Those who do witness are often the new Christians who are highly motivated because of the recent revolution that has taken place in their lives. But the so-called "mature" believers tend to lose this edge. Richard Lovelace describes the scenario this way in his book *Dynamics of Spiritual Life*:

> The "ultimate concern" of most church members is not the worship and service of Christ in evangelistic mission and social compassion, but rather survival and success in their secular vocation. The church is a spoke on the wheel of life connected to the secular hub. It is a departmental subconcern, not the organizing center of all other concerns. Church members who have been conditioned all their lives to devote themselves to building their own kingdom and whose flesh naturally gravitates in that direction anyway find it hard to invest much energy in the kingdom of God. They go to church once or twice a

week and punch the clock, so to speak, fulfilling their "church obligation" by sitting
passively and listening critically or approv-
ingly to the pastor's teaching. Sometimes,
with great effort they can be moved into
some active role in the church's program,
like a trained seal in a circus act, but their
hearts are not fully in it. . . . Their understanding of sin focuses upon behavioral externals which they can eliminate from
their lives by a little willpower and ignores
the great submerged continents of pride,
covetousness and hostility beneath the
surface. Thus their pharisaism defends
them both against full involvement in the
church's mission and against full subjec-
tion of their inner lives to the authority of
Christ.[3]

Dr. Lovelace is saying that the powerful dynamic
of the Holy Spirit and the peace He brings should
motivate us to live by faith and share our faith. But
we are often too wrapped up in the things of this
world to the extent that we don't have the time or the
passion to care or share.

Acts 1:8 tells us that the believer receives power
when he becomes a follower of Christ. So we cannot be excused for the lack of *power* to witness. We
have every imaginable booklet, pamphlet and training tool at our disposal. Therefore, no one can
blame a shortage of outreach on a dearth of *information*. And still, many pastors and church leaders

cannot remember the last time they shared the gospel of Jesus with anyone. What's wrong with this picture?

It is clear that all of us need to get back to the basics of our faith and rediscover all that God has done and what He wants to do. This is what the Savior meant in His sermon to Sardis: "Remember, therefore, what you have received and heard; obey it, and repent" (Revelation 3:3).

This is the essence of genuine revival in the church. It is not about gaining new information. Renewal comes to those who gain a new appreciation for what has already taken place! We need to remember our lives "B.C." ("before Christ") and then be blessed by our fulfillment "A.D." ("after dedication" to Him). As leaders come to terms with this, the people will be blessed, too. But if we don't experience renewal, the church will not be moved.

Peacemakers: False and True

Christ was aware of the fact that there will always be false peacemakers and prophets in our midst, so He offered this warning:

> Watch out for false prophets. They come to you in sheep's clothing, but inwardly they are ferocious wolves. By their fruit you will recognize them. Do people pick grapes from thornbushes, or figs from thistles? Likewise every good tree bears good fruit, but a bad tree bears bad fruit. A good tree cannot bear bad fruit, and a bad tree cannot bear good fruit. . . . Thus, by

their fruit you will recognize them. (Matthew 7:15-18, 20)

This illustration was especially poignant for the Jews. It was a familiar image. Old Testament prophets could be easily identified because they wore sheepskin garments. So false prophets recognized a way to make a fast buck by dressing in the same manner. Townspeople would come to them for advice or a sermon and then pay them. In reality, these slippery charlatans were just covetous wolves in sheepskin jackets.

So how can we tell the true from the false? A true peacemaker can be recognized by the evidence of godliness in his or her life—in other words, the good fruit. This is a person who walks the walk of peace, who is a living demonstration of the inner tranquility that only God can produce. Although "peace" is just one of the aspects of the fruit of the Spirit, it is used here to illustrate the overall control of the Holy Spirit in the peacemaker's life. Perhaps Jesus chose peace because He understands about people and relationships. So many human relationships are filled with strife and He comes as the peace giver for all human relationships as well as the peacemaker between God and man.

Christ says that we are to carefully observe and listen to those who claim to be peacemakers. Is it really a message of peace? Are they really demonstrating this in their lifestyles? We must be discerning because it is so easy to be fooled.

Many who seek church leadership positions put on a good front prior to the elections. But once they are on the board, the wolf inside starts to bark and bite. It becomes clear that their agenda was not peace at all. They love division and contention. The bigger the fight, the better! David Johnson discusses this danger:

> Some churches are as dysfunctional as some family systems. Some of those who are elected to be leaders are carnal, whining, immature babies who wouldn't recognize the work of God if it bit them on the nose! How did they get into leadership positions? The peacekeepers must always make sure that these domineering troublemakers are placated. No one ever confronts them with their childishness because they don't want to stir up trouble. So we will be selective about whose sin we will confront. We must make sure that we keep the peace with the power people. Just keep the peace.[4]

Notice the distinction being made here between "peacemaker" and "peacekeeper." Peace*keepers* are committed to making everybody happy. "Don't upset the apple cart" is their modus operandi. Such people are unwilling to confront sin. They settle for temporary solutions and pseudo-peace. Peace*makers*, on the other hand, are ready and willing to do whatever it takes to make real, lasting harmony.

Christ goes on to say that grapes are not gathered from thorn bushes. There is a thornbush that grows in Israel which has little clusters of purple berries. They look very much like grapes, but they are inedible. In fact, they are bitter. A thistle tree also flourishes in that part of the world which has blossoms that resemble ripe figs. Once again, it is an optical illusion. The message is apparent: we are to closely inspect those who are bringing us so-called messages from God and who seek leadership in the church. Their lives should be marked by peace with God and their lifestyle must be marked by relationships with the lost, whom they are seeking to bring to peace with God.

Jesus further illustrates the distinction between false and true peacemakers:

> Not everyone who says to me, "Lord, Lord," will enter the kingdom of heaven, but only he who does the will of my Father who is in heaven. Many will say to me on that day, "Lord, Lord, did we not prophesy in your name, and in your name drive out demons and perform many miracles?" Then I will tell them plainly, "I never knew you. Away from me, you evildoers!" (Matthew 7:21-23)

We are warned again about the impostors who will come along with the finest of religious trappings. Many will try to imitate the power of God with signs and miracles. This happened in Jesus' day among pseudo-"faith healers" who preyed on those who had psychosomatic illnesses. These bogus prophets would pretend to cast out the demons that caused the sickness. It provided a certain emotional and psychological lift for the patient, and then they claimed to have been healed.

Christ did not have to denounce these false prophets by name. He just demonstrated the real thing by genuinely healing the sick and bringing sight back to the blind. He taught with an authority that was unparalleled. The most learned scholars and intellectuals of His day could not outwit Him. Jesus was and is the "real deal." And we can know the genuine from the imitation among His followers, too.

Perhaps there is no more final statement in all of the world than for God to say to an individual, "I do not know you." We are aware of the fact that the Creator made each of us. He saw our unformed body parts before we even came into being (Psalm 139). But those who have disobeyed God and lived for themselves are in for a rude awakening someday. The One who made them will disown them. Truly this is the definition of hell.

"Blessed are the peacemakers, for they will be called sons of God" (Matthew 5:9). Jesus is drawing a subtle distinction here. There are those of whom He will say, "I never knew you." Then there are those who are "called the children of God"—i.e., people who are known by God. We are heirs, together with Christ, of all that the heavenly Father has for us as His children.

Make the Peace

We are called as church leaders to be peacemakers by living out the peace of God as children of

God. The Lord wants to use us as His instrument to draw others into the family. This is making peace. We become a tool of reconciliation between God and man, even as our Lord did on the cross.

So many of the tools we have for leading people to peace with God have been what I call reaping tools. They are geared to assist people in leading those who are already prepared to receive Christ. We have left out the training for people to learn to cultivate relationships with the lost and to bring God into that relationship through godly love and intentional conversations. As leaders we need to be modeling the habit of making friends with the lost and assisting others to do the same.

Not only can we be used to bring peace between people and Christ, but we can also be used to make peace between man and man, woman and woman, man and woman. Though we may feel inadequate to jump into the fray of human conflict, the God of peace will be our strength.

How will people know that they can trust us to help them resolve a dispute? They will see our total submission to and absolute dependence upon God. They will observe the grace, mercy and peace which we are experiencing. Ultimately, it is not our clever skills for resolving conflict that will make the difference. The Lord Jesus is the reconciler. We just need to be prayerful and careful to listen to God and those in need.

Peace is a wonderful environment for building spiritual depth and numerical growth in the church. Consider the testimony of the early church: "Then the church throughout Judea, Galilee and Samaria enjoyed a time of peace. It was strengthened; and encouraged by the Holy Spirit, it grew in numbers, living in the fear of the Lord" (Acts 9:31).

In this sense, the pastor and leaders of any congregation need to "lead in peace." Defend the peace of God in the fellowship of believers! Why? Because a skeptical world is watching. The congregation in conflict loses its evangelistic power and authority in the community.

Humble, broken, submissive, dependent, merciful, pure, peacemaking—this is not the list of leadership qualities you will find in a *secular* book! But should we really be surprised? Christ's kingdom is not of this world. It's a whole new way of leading.

The Master offers two more character traits of the biblical leader.

⚜ LEADERSHIP REFLECTIONS

1. The average church in America leads less than one person to Christ every year. How are you doing on your leadership team in modeling cultivating relationships with the lost, planting Christ into your lost friends' lives and bringing them to Him?
2. How does the peace and joy among your leadership and in your congregation impact your community for Christ?

LEADERSHIP PRINCIPLE

8

PERSEVERANCE

THE GODLY LEADER IS empowered by the Holy Spirit to face persecution and remain faithful, thus being an example to those who follow.

Chapter
EIGHT

Testing One, Two, Three

Blessed are you when people insult you, persecute you and falsely say all kinds of evil against you because of me. Rejoice and be glad, because great is your reward in heaven, for in the same way they persecuted the prophets who were before you. (Matthew 5:11-12)

Augustine once said, "The same stroke which crushes the straw, separates the pure grain which the Lord has chosen." Indeed, persecution may destroy that which is not pure and holy in the church. But at the same time, times of trouble will also reveal all that is of Christ in His church.

The reality of persecution is a recurring theme with New Testament writers and our Lord Himself. The Apostle Peter told us that we should not be shocked at all when we suffer for the Savior:

Dear friends, do not be surprised at the painful trial you are suffering, as though something strange were happening to you. But rejoice that you participate in the sufferings of Christ, so that you may be overjoyed when his glory is revealed. (1 Peter 4:12-13)

Paul said "Amen" to this in his second letter to Timothy: "Everyone who wants to live a godly life in Christ Jesus will be persecuted" (3:12).

In John 15, Jesus added some details to the beatitude in Matthew 5:

> If the world hates you, keep in mind that it hated me first. If you belonged to the world, it would love you as its own. As it is, you do not belong to the world, but I have chosen you out of the world. That is why the world hates you. Remember the words I spoke to you: "No servant is greater than his master." If they persecuted me, they will persecute you also. If they obeyed my teaching, they will obey yours also. They will treat you this way because of my name, for they do not know the One who sent me. (John 15:18-21)

Simply defined, "persecution" means to be attacked for the purpose of being driven away. This is the result of the world's hatred for God. We become "guilty by association." As we represent Christ ever more faithfully, we will be rejected more consistently, too. David Johnson puts it this way:

> To persecute means "to chase, to pursue, to harass." And you don't have to be nailed to a cross or shot with an arrow to feel that tension. You will understand what it means

to be reviled because that is defined as "having something thrown in your face." You'll be made fun of, and others will speak falsely of you in evil ways. They will slander behind your back.

This is what happens when the kingdom comes to us. We become broken people who know how to mourn. Then we see with new eyes that it will be the pure in heart who will see the kingdom. This gives us a new mouth to say what we saw. And when we get persecuted for that, we are in real good company! We must be doing something right.[1]

I am convinced that we have limited our discussion of this subject because of a very basic, human fear: If we talk about it, we just might experience more of it! But this avoidance tactic cannot change the profound fact that our alliance with a holy God will put us at odds with sinful people both inside and outside the church. We must accept this reality as leaders so that we can be prepared personally, but also so that we can prepare others for the assault that *will* come.

Suffering for the Right Reason

God blesses those who are persecuted *because they live for God*. There are many Christians who bring oppression upon themselves through behavior that is extremely objectionable. Peter expressed it this way: "If you suffer, it should not be as a murderer or thief or any other kind of criminal, or even as a meddler" (1 Peter 4:15).

Some who would call themselves believers have bombed abortion clinics in the name of Christ. Abortionists have been murdered by those who say they are acting on orders from God. When caught and imprisoned, they claim to be experiencing Matthew 5:10-12. Nothing could be further from the truth. This is self-inflicted persecution; it does not further the kingdom of God in any way.

Jesus did not say, "Blessed are those who are oppressed because they have broken the law." Fulfillment does not come for those who behave in a radical, violent manner and become obnoxious in the eyes of the legal system. The Savior is talking exclusively about "suffering for the sake of righteousness."

David Johnson has something to say about this as well:

> We sometimes confuse a false persecution with the real thing. For instance, sometimes our presentation of Christ to the world is not in the context of brokenness and mourning. It's not about a real hunger and thirst for God. Rather, we may confront the world with our spiritual arrogance, religious superiority and legalistic rigidity. Then we get reviled for being rigid, superior and condescending, and we call that "being persecuted for righteousness." Let's not call it that because this is not what Christ was talking about. Matthew 5:10-12 applies

only to that persecution which results from the lifestyle of Matthew 5:3-9.[2]

Some years ago, there was a radio ministry that spoke very forcefully against communism in the name of Christianity. This group accused several contemporary politicians of being actual or closet communists, pronouncing doom and disaster on these "enemies of America." When their broadcast licenses were revoked, they claimed that they were being "persecuted for righteousness' sake."

Though these folks may have had good intentions, they were fighting the wrong fight. The righteousness of Christ was not the issue. An overemphasis on political ideology had led them to bad theology. Their belligerence and negative tone reduced the impact that they could have made for the gospel's sake.

Persecution should not be the result of a cause around which we are rallying. Jesus said that we will be reviled for choosing to live in a godly manner. His righteousness displayed in our daily lives will lead others to despise us. It is not a matter of the views we espouse, or the groups with which we are aligned. Our pursuit of Christlikeness will put us at odds with those who want to go their own way.

External Persecution

Persecution generally falls into two categories: *external* and *internal*. External suffering is that which comes from without or from the world. This is effectively illustrated by a story from Nehemiah's life in chapter 4 of his book. He was a "cupbearer" for the king. We would call him a "taste-tester" today.

Whenever King Artaxerxes was served a drink, Nehemiah would take the first swallow.

However, the cupbearer was not just a beverage-sipping servant. This was a highly esteemed position in the parliament. Nehemiah was in constant communication with the sovereign; thus it was easy for him to talk with the king and gain favors from him. Many of these servants were very wealthy just because of their close ties with royalty.

God spoke to Nehemiah about his responsibility to rebuild the broken-down walls of the city of Jerusalem. Eventually, the servant's burden became apparent to the king because of their close relationship. Artaxerxes came right out with it: "Why does your face look so sad when you are not ill? This can be nothing but sadness of heart" (Nehemiah 2:2).

Nehemiah lamented over the desperate conditions of his people back in Jerusalem. They were starving; the city was in ruins. The king immediately gave orders to give his cupbearer everything he needed to go to Jerusalem so that he could bring healing to the people and repair the crumbling walls and buildings.

But a number of the rulers in nearby territories were extremely upset with this action taken by King Artaxerxes. As the Jews began to rebuild the walls and fortify the city of Jerusalem, persecution came upon those who were simply doing what God had asked them to do.

> When Sanballat heard that we were rebuilding the wall, he became angry and was

greatly incensed. He ridiculed the Jews, and in the presence of his associates and the army of Samaria, he said, "What are these feeble Jews doing? Will they restore their wall? Will they offer sacrifices? Will they finish in a day? Can they bring the stones back to life from those heaps of rubble— burned as they are?

Tobiah the Ammonite, who was at his side, said, "What they are building—if even a fox climbed up on it, he would break down their wall of stones!" (Nehemiah 4:1-3)

Sanballat and Tobiah were expressing their scorn at the notion that it was possible for the Jews to accomplish God's will. And many times in our lives, persecution will take this form. People will say things like, "What in the world do you think you're doing? Those are stupid decisions you are making! How will you ever make a living if you follow where the Lord is leading you?"

But the key to the story is that Nehemiah and the people were doing what God had told them to do— and they were courageous enough to believe that they would be blessed for their efforts. Though Sanballat, Tobiah and others attacked them and attempted to break down the rebuilt wall, God's people went forward in spite of such persecution. This story illustrates the way that church leaders will sometimes be scorned, shunned and abused by those outside the fellowship who want to mock the work of the Lord.

The body of Christ has also suffered external persecution in the form of physical torture and martyrdom. William Barclay reminds us that:

> Nero wrapped the Christians in pitch and set them alight and used them as living torches to light his gardens. He sewed them in the skins of wild animals and set his hunting dogs upon them to tear them to death. They were tortured on the rack, they were scraped with pinchers; molten lead was poured hissing upon them; red hot brass plates were affixed to the tenderest parts of their bodies; eyes were torn out; parts of their bodies were cut off and roasted before their eyes; their hands and feet were burned while cold water was poured over them to lengthen the agony. These things are not pleasant to think about, but these are the things a man had to be prepared for, if he took his stand with Jesus Christ.[3]

How could Christians withstand this intense persecution and even forgive the perpetrators? Because like their Master as He was crucified and Stephen as he was being stoned, they realized that their tormentors did not understand what they were doing (see Luke 23:34 and Acts 7:60).

Internal Persecution

External persecution may be easier to understand. Unbelievers do not have the advantage of knowing our great God's forgiveness and cleansing. They will hate us for our happiness and sense of fulfillment.

But there is another kind of suffering that is more difficult to understand. Look at Nehemiah 5:

> Now the men and their wives raised a great outcry against their Jewish brothers. Some were saying, "We and our sons and daughters are numerous; in order for us to eat and stay alive, we must get grain."
>
> Others were saying, "We are mortgaging our fields, our vineyards and our homes to get grain during the famine." (Nehemiah 5:1-3)

Clearly, these were difficult times for the Jewish people. As they gave all of their time and energy to rebuilding the walls, the rich landowners were buying up their fields and vineyards. These profiteers would then sell the produce from these crops back to the people at exorbitant prices. Some of the families had to sell their sons and daughters into slavery just to survive.

Nehemiah became aware of these injustices and told the landowners that this abuse could not continue. They were supposed to be working together in doing God's will. The rich should have been sharing with the poor. The cupbearer ordered them to give the property back to the people and return family members who had been sold as slaves. Nehemiah called on them to begin looking out for each other in a team effort to rebuild Jerusalem.

This is an example of the persecution that can come from within the body of Christ. Unfortunately, there are those in the Christian community who would take advantage of others who want to walk in obedience to the Lord. A careful study of the life of Christ reveals that the vast majority of His suffering came at the hands of the traditional religious community.

Much of the oppression in the church today is also *internal*. From within the very body of Christ, there will be those who want to disrupt and corrupt in pursuit of a self-centered agenda. This is why it is imperative for church leaders to have character that has been formed from within by the indwelling Christ.

Leaders will be called upon to discern the truth and walk in it. As we pursue godliness, it will not be unusual for us to be ostracized by other believers. Though we may not face the same level of persecution suffered by those in the early church, we will still experience this to some degree.

William Barclay explains the issues faced by leaders who chose to walk with the Lord in those days shortly after the Savior's ascension:

> It's hard for us to realize what the first Christians had to suffer. Every department of their life was disrupted. Their Christianity might well disrupt their work. Suppose a man was a stone mason. That seems like a harmless enough occupation. But suppose his firm received a contract to build a temple to one of the heathen gods, what was that man to do? Suppose a man was a tailor, and suppose his firm was asked to produce robes for the heathen priests, what was that

man to do? In a situation such as that in which the early Christians found themselves, there was hardly any job in which a man might not find conflict between his business interests and his loyalty to Jesus Christ. The church was in no doubt where a man's duty lay. More than a hundred years after this, a man came to Tertullian with this very problem. He told of his business difficulties. He ended by saying, "What can I do? I must live." "Must you?" said Tertullian. If it came to a choice between loyalty and a living, the real Christian never hesitated to choose loyalty.[4]

Mr. Barclay goes on to describe the impact on the believer's social life:

In the ancient world, most feasts were held in the temple of some god. In very few sacrifices was the whole animal burned upon the altar. It might be that only a few hairs from the forehead of the beast were burned as a symbolic sacrifice. Part of the meat went to the priests as their perquisite; and part of the meat was returned to the worshiper. With his share, he made a feast for his friends and relations. One of the gods most commonly worshiped was Serapis. And when the invitations to the feast went out, they would read: "I invite you to dine with me at the table of our lord, Serapis." Could a Christian share in a feast held in the

temple of a heathen god? . . . Could a Christian become a sharer in a heathen act of
worship like that? Again, the Christian's answer was clear. The Christian must cut himself off from his fellows rather than by his
presence give approval of such a thing.[5]

But perhaps the most challenging aspect of their
commitment to God was the way in which it dis-
rupted their family life. Barclay continues:

It happened again and again that one
member of a family became a Christian
while the others did not. A wife might become a Christian while her husband did
not. A son or daughter might become a
Christian while the rest of the family did
not. Immediately there was a split in the
family. Often the door was shut forever in
the face of the one who had accepted Christ.
. . . It was literally true that a man might
have to love Christ more than a father or
mother, wife or brother or sister.[6]

So how does this work in the contemporary
church? Leaders can expect to be persecuted by
slander. People will indeed speak all manner of evil
against the leader who takes a stand for righteousness. False rumors will be started even among those
who name the name of Christ. Motives will be mis-
interpreted to make a pastor or an elder look bad.

Over the years I have noticed some of the classic
attacks that occur in the church. One of the most difficult to deal with is the "our pastor is not feeding us

anymore" syndrome. This is to say that the person speaking no longer appreciates the messages being preached. The difficulty with this perspective is that nowhere in Scripture is the pastor told to "feed" the sheep—at least, not in the way these critics use the word. The job of the pastor is to lead the sheep to quiet waters and green pastures so they can feed themselves. Sheep who are fed like cows in a barn do not stay healthy any more than believers who rely on the Sunday message for their spiritual food.

Other common attacks are to switch the leader's words around and question his integrity. Anyone who speaks publicly not only will misspeak from time to time but will be misunderstood. I once pastored a church where the previous pastor was what I called a "hugger." He hugged everyone as they went out the door on Sunday morning. Because I was not a "hugger," I was accused of not loving the people.

A pastor friend of mine told me of a few board members in a church he had served who were regularly hinting negatively about the amount of his salary. The obvious implication was that the minister must be a greedy, materialistic man if he makes that kind of money. The remuneration was not exorbitant by any stretch of the imagination, but the pastor still had to deal with the innuendo of avarice.

Leaders of the flock of God can expect direct, verbal abuse. We will experience things like this because the slave is not greater than the Master. Even as our Lord suffered at the hands of respected religious figures, we, too, will face some of our staunchest opposi-

tion at the hands of those who attend church, sing all
the right songs and quote all the right verses.

Our Lord must have had these painful realities in
mind as He proclaimed to His future leaders,
"Blessed are those who are persecuted for the sake of
righteousness."

The character that can withstand such suffering is
formed by the Holy Spirit as He does His work of humility, brokenness, submission and dependence
within us. As this work progresses, it produces a
leader who guides others with mercy. He seeks holiness and makes every attempt to be a peacemaker.
Dependence on Christ provides endurance for leaders to stand up for Him in the midst of persecution.

Responding to Persecution

The question begs an answer: "How should we
respond to persecution?"

Jesus gives us the answer in Matthew 5:12, but it is
not the one we will like: *Be happy about it! Be very glad!*
Now *that* is an interesting reaction to suffering! But
He clarifies just why this should be our disposition:
For a great reward awaits you in heaven. This means that
when we are oppressed for righteousness' sake, the
blessings of God's kingdom will be ours to enjoy, in
part, right here and right now. If we are willing to live
all for Jesus, we will be persecuted. But we will also
know the benediction of the Father.

But blessings are not the only dividend of suffering. In addition, we will literally receive payment in
the heavenlies. The first installment is enjoyed here
by getting to know the Lord in more intimate ways

than we could have if we had not been oppressed. The final payoff will come in heaven itself when "we shall be like [Christ], for we shall see him as he is" (1 John 3:2).

There is no greater reward for the servant of God. What must it be like to completely know God in His fullness and to be known by Him? The same almighty Creator who fashioned this universe with the wink of His eye is the same God who wants us to comprehend Him thoroughly. This is why we can rejoice and be glad in the midst of persecution—we have the glorious hope of someday knowing our precious Lord without reservation.

Just think of the great men and women of the faith alluded to in the word, "prophets" (Matthew 5:12). A partial list is given to us in Hebrews 11. The point is that *we* can be included with these dear saints who knew the hardships associated with following God wholeheartedly. What a joy to be part of God's "in" crowd! This is good company indeed!

Persecution's Product

The concluding verses of the "Greatest Leadership Training Seminar on Earth" go much further than to just illustrate that persecution is coming. We can be prepared to deal with suffering when it comes.

> Therefore everyone who hears these words of mine and puts them into practice is like a wise man who built his house on the rock. The rain came down, the streams rose, and the winds blew and beat against that

house; yet it did not fall, because it had its foundation on the rock. (Matthew 7:24-25)

So if we hear the word of God and do something about it in our daily lives, we will be able to withstand even hurricane-force oppression without crumbling. We have our Lord's promise and He is trustworthy. Built upon the solid foundation of Christ's righteousness, we will be unshakable.

Jesus goes on in the next two verses to say,

But everyone who hears these words of mine and does not put them into practice is like a foolish man who built his house on sand. The rain came down, the streams rose, and the winds blew and beat against that house, and it fell with a great crash. (7:26-27)

"With a great crash" means that those who disregard Christ will fall. If there are "levels" of hell, perhaps the worst will be reserved for those who were fully aware of the truth but rejected it in favor of rebellion.

So here are our choices: We can hear, obey and walk with God both now and forever, or we can hear, disobey and spend eternity separated from Him. Although following Him here and now will most definitely lead to suffering, it will also lead to blessings here and hereafter. The persecution is temporal. The other pathway is easier in some ways on this earth, but leads to eternal suffering.

When leaders are able to both "persevere" and "rejoice" in the midst of suffering, it is evidence of a deep work of the Holy Spirit on the inside. There is nothing in the human disposition which allows us to experience joy in the midst of difficult times. But by God's power and grace, we can know contentment in our calamity.

As our understanding of the Lord and godly leadership deepens, we become more aware of this simple fact: *We can do literally nothing apart from the Lord Jesus.* Only as His character is being reproduced in us can we hope to guide the church past this crisis of non-growth. Only as we become Christlike will we be able to lead the body of Christ into a future of God-ordained growth both spiritually and numerically as He adds daily those who believe.

And that leads us to the summary goal of leaders: *Christlikeness.*

LEADERSHIP REFLECTIONS

1. What circumstances have caused you to grow in perseverance? What do we learn from how Jesus dealt with persecution that applies to us today?
2. Develop a set of guidelines for how your leadership and church will deal with gossip, slander and other types of attacks on the church.

CHRISTLIKENESS

THE DISCIPLED CHURCH LEADER is Christ-like in that he is the salt of the earth and the light of the world. As a result, he will be a witness of and to the things of God.

CHAPTER
nine

Oh, to Be Like Him!

You are the salt of the earth. But if the salt loses its saltiness, how can it be made salty again? It is no longer good for anything, except to be thrown out and trampled by men.

You are the light of the world. A city on a hill cannot be hidden. Neither do people light a lamp and put it under a bowl. Instead they put it on its stand, and it gives light to everyone in the house. In the same way, let your light shine before men, that they may see your good deeds and praise your Father in heaven. (Matthew 5:13-16)

The first twelve verses of Matthew chapter 5, have given us a character analysis of the person who would be a leader in the church. These principles of leadership have been illustrated by practical application to life situations in the balance of the Sermon on the Mount. We come now to what we will consider as the last few statements in Jesus' message to His future leaders.

Christ is announcing that as a result of the work of God in their lives, they are to be the salt of the earth and the light of the world. These verses are perhaps the most important in the entire chapter because they give us a glimpse of the Lord's "big picture" for our lives. We are called to be like Christ.

It was Thomas O. Chisholm who penned this famous hymn:

> Oh, to be like Thee! blessed Redeemer,
> This is my constant longing and prayer.
> Gladly I'll forfeit all of earth's treasures,
> Jesus, Thy perfect likeness to wear.
> Oh, to be like Thee, Oh, to be like Thee,
> Blessed Redeemer, pure as Thou art!
> Come in Thy sweetness, come in Thy
>   fullness;
> Stamp Thine own image deep on my
>   heart.[1]

How can a hymn like this be fulfilled in our lives? As we become salt and light.

Salt That Preserves

One of the primary uses for salt is, of course, as a preservative. It prevents things from decaying. For instance, we know what happens to a piece of raw meat that lies on a counter during the summertime; within a few hours, it becomes repulsive and rotten. Salted meat, however, has a much longer shelf life.

Jesus called His followers "salt" to suggest that the world is in a state of moral and spiritual putrefaction. In Genesis 6, God looked at the human race and gave this dim assessment to Noah:

> Now the earth was corrupt in God's
> sight and was full of violence. God saw
> how corrupt the earth had become, for all
> the people on earth had corrupted their
> ways. So God said to Noah, "I am going to
> put an end to all people, for the earth is
> filled with violence because of them. I am
> surely going to destroy both them and the
> earth." (Genesis 6:11-13)

This description in the first book of the Bible is not
unlike the portrayal of the world by implication in
Matthew 5. The violence and evil of society in
Noah's day induced God to destroy it. In Jesus' day,
the Father saw the pharisaical religiosity of those who
claimed to know Him. So He sent His only Son to
rescue as many as possible through His sacrifice on
the cross.

The Role of the Holy Spirit

Today, as followers of Christ, we have been sent by
God to be the salt of the earth in the place of our
Lord. We are to offer the message of hope and salva-
tion while the Creator allows us to be that preserva-
tive which will keep the world from decaying. A.T.
Pierson says it this way:

> The Spirit of God, the *Paraclete*, is to be to
> the disciple and to the church all that Christ
> would have been had He tarried among us
> and been the personal companion and
> counselor of each and all. And by the Spirit
> of God working in and through the believer

and the church, believers are, in their measure, to be to the world what the Spirit is to them.[2]

By being salt, then, we become by His Spirit what Christ would have been if He had continued to live on this earth. This is applicable to all believers, but it is imperative for church leadership. And Pierson points out a principle of utmost importance. We are not called to be salt in our own power and strength. In Acts 1:8, Jesus told His future leaders to wait until the Holy Spirit came upon them. He would indwell them and empower them for effective ministry.

As leaders in His church today, we, too, must be filled with the Spirit. This is often an area of great misunderstanding. Misconceptions abound. Many Christians think that the third Person of the Trinity just pushes us along in our daily walk, trying to get us to obey God. But there is much more to it that this!

In the Gospel of John, we have the statements of Jesus with regard to the function of the Holy Spirit. This beautifully summarizes His work in us as we become the salt of the earth:

> And I will ask the Father, and he will give you another Counselor to be with you forever—the Spirit of truth. The world cannot accept him, because it neither sees him nor knows him. But you know him, for he lives with you and will be in you. . . .
>
> All this I have spoken while still with you. But the Counselor, the Holy Spirit, whom

the Father will send in my name, will teach you all things and will remind you of everything I have said to you. . . .

When the Counselor comes, whom I will send to you from the Father, the Spirit of truth who goes out from the Father, he will testify about me. And you also must testify, for you have been with me from the beginning. . . .

But I tell you the truth: It is for your good that I am going away. Unless I go away, the Counselor will not come to you; but if I go, I will send him to you. When he comes, he will convict the world of guilt in regard to sin and righteousness and judgment: in regard to sin, because men do not believe in me; in regard to righteousness, because I am going to the Father, where you can see me no longer; and in regard to judgment, because the prince of this world now stands condemned.

I have much more to say to you, more than you can now bear. But when he, the Spirit of truth, comes, he will guide you into all truth. He will not speak on his own; he will speak only what he hears, and he will tell you what is yet to come. He will bring glory to me by taking from what is mine and making it known to you. All that belongs to the Father is mine. That is why I said the Spirit will take from what is mine and make it known to you. (John 14:16-17, 25-26; 15:26-27; 16:7-15)

First, we see that He is the Counselor (14:16) or *Paraclete*. Pierson gives this definition:

> This word "paraclete" . . . seems to embody mainly the conception of being called to one's aid or summoned to act as a substitute. . . . Whatever other conceptions may properly pertain to the name Paraclete, this seems to be central and controlling: The Holy Spirit comes when Christ goes—comes to take the place of the absent Lord Jesus; to become, therefore, to the believer and to the church as the collective body of believers all that Christ would have been had he remained on earth.[3]

The implication of this definition is clear: the Spirit of our Lord Jesus is to be to us all that Jesus Himself was to His followers. We need to take advantage of His wise counsel and guidance through the Word and prayer if we plan to be the "salt of the earth."

A second thing we notice in John's record is that the Spirit is "the Spirit of truth" (14:17), who will "teach [us] all things" (14:26). In fact, the Holy Spirit will give us the words for witnessing (15:26-27). John 16:13-15 further amplifies the Spirit's skill as our guide into all truth by citing His constant source: Christ Himself. We can be confident that the Holy Spirit will always speak as Jesus would speak. We also know that Jesus always spoke the words of the Father (John 17:7). Therefore, the sayings of the Spirit are always the message of God the Father, too.

Is it any wonder that Jesus instructed His disciples to wait for the infilling of the Spirit before they attempted to be "salt and light" for God's kingdom? This wonderful Paraclete is our source of truth and testimony. In this day of cults and false teaching, we need to lean more heavily on this promise from the Lord Jesus. We cannot be salt for the Savior apart from our total reliance on the Spirit of truth.

In John 14:17, we receive this incredible promise: "he [the Holy Spirit] lives with you and will be in you."

When we come to know Jesus Christ as Savior and Lord, our sins are washed away and we are reconciled to God. But that's not all! Jesus puts within us the very Spirit of the living God to empower us for His service! When our Master walked this earth, He was unable to always be with those He was training because of the limitations of a physical body. But today, we have the glorious advantage of having His Spirit *dwelling within us*!

God's Spirit is always there to be drawn upon for wisdom in confusing circumstances, comfort in times of sorrow, rejoicing in victories and power for serving the Lord more effectively. This is the life of salt and light which draws men, women and young people to Christ.

Leaders as Salt

In Micah 5:7, we read, "The remnant of Jacob will be in the midst of many peoples like dew from the LORD, like showers on the grass, which do not wait for man or linger for mankind."

God was pointing out through His prophet that there would always be a remnant of people to share this good news. Anyone who accepts the gospel of God and lives by faith will escape the decay of this world. The church and its leaders have proven this to be true.

People all around us are asking the basic questions of life:

"Why am I here?"

"Where am I going?"

"How can I find meaning and happiness?"

Christians are the only people in this world who have reasonable answers to those questions. Indeed, we are here for the express purpose of demonstrating that life can be fulfilling in the "nasty here and now," along with the fact that there is hope for a bright future in the "sweet by and by." We serve as a preservative which can stop the decaying influence of this world's system by embracing new life in Christ.

Notice the words "You are . . ." in Matthew 5:13. Those whose character is being shaped by Matthew 5:1-12 "are" in the process of becoming Christlike. This is a simple statement of fact. It is not debatable.

Yet as we look at the contemporary church of Jesus Christ in North America, these bedrock principles of godly leadership have obviously been ignored, overlooked or misunderstood. Regardless of denominational affiliation, congregation after congregation is struggling because we have gotten away from these basics.

In, but Not Of

When people come to know Christ as their Savior, they begin to enjoy the fellowship of the body of Christ. But so often, they find themselves being cut off from non-Christian friends. They develop a new lifestyle that may isolate them from those who need the Lord. And it is necessary for the believer to leave the *ways* of the world. But it is absolutely contrary to God's Word to abandon the *people* of the world.

In John 17, Jesus discusses this issue in great detail:

> I have given them your word and the world has hated them, for they are not of the world any more than I am of the world. My prayer is not that you take them out of the world but that you protect them from the evil one. They are not of the world, even as I am not of it. Sanctify them by the truth; your word is truth. (John 17:14-17)

In a phrase, Christ tells us that our relationship with the world should go like this: "In it, but not of it." He goes a step further to establish the fact that He has sent believers into the world even as He was sent on a mission to our world from His Father. And we are sent into society to live a holy and righteous life. We can demonstrate how we can be reconciled to God and live in a state of peace and rest while the culture all around us is in constant turmoil.

Note again that we do not *become* the salt of the
earth—we *are* the salt! It is our Lord's expectation
that we will be involved in our society. Implicit is the
understanding that we will both "walk the walk and
talk the talk" of Christianity that will draw people
like a magnet to the Savior.

The mission of the church—to make disciples of
Jesus Christ—is therefore binding on every believer.
It is not exclusively a "missionary" thing for an out-
post in some faraway country. Each of us has been
called to be the salt of the earth in our sphere of influence. We do not have the same gifts or tasks in the
body of Christ, but we do have a common purpose:
to preserve our culture from moral and spiritual decay through a living demonstration of the new birth.

This requires action on our part. Church leaders
who are not meeting this standard of "salt and light"
in Christlikeness are going to find it very difficult to
give direction to a congregation that needs to grow
spiritually and numerically. The deep work of the
Spirit must be accomplished in the life of any shepherd before he can lead the flock of God. Only then is
any person qualified to give guidance to the body of
Christ.

Tasteless Salt

With complete candor, the Master states that
when salt becomes tasteless, it has no use whatsoever—it should be thrown away. The salt used in Jesus' day was often impure. It was necessary to
separate that which was pure and potent from that
which was unable to provide protection against de-

cay. This refining process left a look-alike residue that was tasteless. Because the remaining substance was essentially useless, the "pseudo-salt" was scattered in the temple courts much like we might use sawdust today.

Jesus was speaking to His leaders about the quality of their "saltiness." A paraphrase of Matthew 5:13 might look like this: "You are the salt of the earth, but if your spiritual life has become apathetic and you only possess a look-alike Christianity, then you are of little use in the kingdom of God."

This is quite a warning. Believers who no longer have the necessary characteristics of salt are of no use to God and His kingdom! We will lack the vital ingredients which will enable us to fulfill our mission.

As we carefully study the teachings of Christ and other New Testament writers, we are struck with the notion that faith is much more than just hopeful belief. It must be the absolute confidence in and reliance upon Christ which produces our complete cooperation. Believers often talk about faith as the cornerstone of Christianity, but faith that is genuine will produce obedience. Or in the words of Paul, "For in the gospel a righteousness from God is revealed, a righteousness that is by faith from first to last, just as it is written: 'The righteous will live by faith' " (Romans 1:17).

We are declared "righteous" by God when we live by faith. No one is going to be called godly because they simply observe the law or live by a certain code of ethics. Genuine righteousness is the result of real faith that has generated obedience.

This has important implications for church leaders. Will God be able to use us if we are just using Him as another crutch to add to our list of things that give us self-confidence? I think not. The message of Paul and Christ is that we do not have faith unless we depend totally on the Lord Jesus, separating ourselves from every other prop offered by our culture and falling on our knees to say, "My only hope is You, Lord."

Such a person will be "salty." He or she will be fit for the Master's use. In the world, but not of it. And the proof of our profession will be this: We will live in a manner that hinders the process of corruption around us.

Leaders as Light

The Savior does not stop with just one analogy to describe the leader's life. He continues in Matthew 5:14 with this startling announcement: *we are the light of the world*! This, of course, infers that the world is presently in a state of darkness. "Darkness" in Scripture is always a symbol of error, sin, guilt, depravity and misery. "Light" is always a symbol of righteousness.

In John 8:12, Jesus stated it this way: "I am the light of the world. Whoever follows me will never walk in darkness, but will have the light of life."

In Ephesians 5, Paul adds, "For you were once darkness, but now you are light in the Lord. Live as children of light" (5:8).

So it is clear that "salt" speaks of who we *are* in our daily lives, while "light" concerns itself with what we are to be *doing*.

It is a frightening prospect to be "the light." Light exposes everything. The light cannot coexist with the dark. As a result, where there is light, darkness cannot be present at the same time. In fact, darkness can only rule in the absence of light.

Have you ever been on a tour through an underground cave? The guide will usually wait until the group has gotten deep below ground level and then say, "OK, everyone turn off your flashlight!" It is an incredible experience of darkness! Unless you have been prepared ahead of time, it can be scary!

Some years ago, I was with some friends hiking through "Hezekiah's Tunnel," located near Jerusalem. We were in a passageway that was just barely wider than our shoulders and at times no more than four or five feet in height. We were walking through water that was ankle deep and ice cold. Suddenly, the only flashlight we had with us blinked out.

We realized that we would have to find our way out of the tunnel with no light whatsoever. The darkness was absolute. All of us had to fight back an overwhelming sense of fear. It seemed that the walls were closing in on us. We wondered if we would ever see the light of day again.

But after twenty minutes of this terror, we saw a thin shaft of light up ahead. There was hope after all! I cannot possibly describe how relieved our group was as we eventually walked back into the daylight.

This is the kind of light that our Lord wants each leader to become. We are to be that glimmer of hope in the darkness. As light, we will lead the church toward to the luminescence of Christ. Jesus is that light. We must guide His people to Him.

Hence, another warning. The Savior tells us that we must never hide the brightness of our love for Him. No one would buy a lamp for his living room and then keep it in the box. Instead, he would put that lamp on a table and turn it on so that everything around the lamp could benefit from the radiance. It would be just as ridiculous for someone, who claimed to be a follower of the One who said, "I am the light of the world," to keep that experience to themselves by hiding it from those who need it.

Either we *are* or we *are not* light. There is no neutral ground here. And if we are His light, it will show: "Let your light shine before men, that they may see your good deeds and praise your Father in heaven" (Matthew 5:16). Note that the command here has to do with the *way* our light shines—not *if* it shines.

What a wonderful light this can be! As we live a life characterized by Matthew 5:1-12, we will be reflecting Christ and His holiness. Our humility, brokenness, submission, dependence, mercy, hunger for righteousness, peacemaking and perseverance will become a floodlight in which others can find their way to a meaningful, joyful Christian walk.

Our society is very offended by those who just "talk the talk" while failing to "walk the walk." But they are also curious about those who live for the Lord without ever *talking* about Him! God is pleased when we combine both walking *and* talking. And none of this is to draw attention to ourselves. We want our words and actions to point everyone to Christ.

Why has God chosen to make His people "light" for the world? Jesus tells us in John 3:

> This is the verdict: Light has come into the world, but men loved darkness instead of light because their deeds were evil. Everyone who does evil hates the light, and will not come into the light for fear that his deeds will be exposed. But whoever lives by the truth comes into the light, so that it may be seen plainly that what he has done has been done through God. (3:19-21)

As we live for the Lord Jesus, our lives become a searchlight that exposes evil. Unbelievers observe our lives and see qualities that are very attractive: peace, joy, real love. They begin to sense that they are in need of a personal relationship with God, too. Then the non-Christian becomes painfully aware that they are "poor in spirit." And so the process begins.

The Creator wisely designed this method for bringing people to the realization of their spiritual bankruptcy. As godly leaders show the way through their own brokenness and humility, others will want to follow.

This is why God is far more interested in building His character into men and women than He is in merely developing programs or reaching goals. True spiritual leaders must be those individuals who are willing to be transformed from the inside out. The Lord accomplishes this through brokenness and blessing, peace and persecution.

A church leader is called to be the salt of the earth and the light of the world. In doing so, he or she will be a witness of and to the things of God. The right kind of church growth occurs when people of Christ-like character live out the truth of God's Word. Church growth that prioritizes the numerical over the spiritual depth of the congregants results in confusion in the world and turmoil in the church.

God wants leaders in His church who are humble, contrite, submissive, dependent, merciful, pure, peaceful and persevering when the going gets rough. Such character builds a man or woman who can become a preservative in a corrupt world. They will be light in the darkest of circumstances, their churches like beacons set on a hill.

In other words, Jehovah wants His leaders to be just like His Son.

✦ LEADERSHIP REFLECTIONS

1. What is the role of the Holy Spirit in our being "salty" leaders to our church?
2. In what practical ways are you as a leadership team being light in your church, your family, your community?

EPILOGUE

New Hope for the Church

Church growth experts agree that leadership is the foundational issue upon which the expansion of congregations in North America depends. The problems associated with non-growing churches are linked primarily to the leaders—whether lay or pastoral. Church leadership authorities have written extensively about the skill development issues inherent in providing effective guidance to a congregation.

In a seminar I attended a few years ago, the speaker made one thing crystal clear: If you do not have a dynamic, visionary, directive style of leadership, some serious soul-searching is required—perhaps a few resignations are even in order. This, the speaker added, is because no church can profit from a senior pastor who does not have his act together with the latest strategies.

The speaker fielded many comments and questions concerning his bold assertions, but he refused to back down even slightly. He continued to defend his conclusions with remarks that led those attending to believe that pastoral leaders with any other style of leadership were actually damaging and restraining the church instead of complementing its growth.

This particular speaker accurately represented the inescapable deductions of the experts in his field. It was all very logical, based on the literature from some corners of the church growth movement. While I can sympathize with many of the tenets of a dynamic, directive, visionary leadership style, I have this nagging sense that there is error here. New hope for the church must never be based on humanistic formulas and stylistic preferences.

Jesus Christ could have chosen only the "dynamic, visionary, directive" types. But He most certainly did not. God could have selected charismatic personalities, but instead He asked for Abraham, Moses and David. These men were not marked by powerful personalities or forceful approaches. On the contrary, they were characterized by their humility, dependence and sense of submission. I contend that any "dynamic, visionary, directive" leader must be branded by Matthew 5 *first* if he or she would be used of God.

This is the *higher standard* to which Jesus wants to call His church. He is less intrigued by our theories of great leadership than we might assume. He is much more interested in our personal and corporate Christlikeness. God seems to consistently choose those who are considered "weak" by this world's measuring stick when He wants to accomplish a great task. This is probably because it is difficult to get the attention of those who have it all together. The self-sufficient soul is not looking for God because they are enamored by their own strengths and abilities.

Leaders in the church today can become so busy with their own agendas that the Master's plans fade into insignificance. According to Psalm 127:1, "Unless the LORD builds the house, its builders labor in vain." This is quite an indictment against many congregations today. For all our money, buildings, programs, personnel, education and "visionary leadership," we still live in a society that is growing increasingly corrupt. The church of Jesus Christ has failed to have a significant impact on the moral climate of our culture.

The Apostle Paul describes our plight well by saying that we have "a form of godliness but [deny] its power" (2 Timothy 3:5). Maybe this is why we have sunk into this impotent state with congregation after congregation reporting decline. Perhaps we have tried to build Christ's church in the energy of the flesh, with the end result that we have *our* church instead of *His* church.

It is time to lead the followers by following the Leader. We must get back to "what [we] have received and heard" (Revelation 3:3). In this case, it would be the inaugural sermon of our Lord and Savior in Matthew 5. We have no choice but to once again embrace the guidelines of Jesus Christ. The church growth movement is right about one thing: Leadership *is* the key to building a growing, dynamic congregation. But they are wrong about the characteristics of those leaders. In fact, it is not even about "characteristics." It's about *character*.

The teaching of the Master in Matthew 5-7 is plain and simple. Church leaders whose lives produce growing congregations are not like the high-powered, "successful" business people who claw their way up the corporate ladder. Rather, they are persons who walk humbly with God and live life in harmony with the principles of godliness. Their lives appear radically different because their priorities are inside out. Godly leaders pay attention first to the inner life.

The Christlike shepherd is not threatened by the qualities listed in Matthew 5, but revels in:

- humility
- brokenness
- submission
- dependence
- mercy
- seeking righteousness
- peacemaking, and
- perseverance.

Such men and women of God recognize that "this world is not their home"—but they bring the kingdom of God to this temporary place of residence as leaders of the church. They know what it is to be comforted and to give comfort, for they have suffered the awareness of their own lostness outside of Christ. Ultimately, these Christlike leaders are not men and women of this world because they have set their sights on an eternal kingdom wherein dwells righteousness.

The *higher standard* church leader chooses to walk with God and is willingly dominated by the Lordship of Jesus Christ. He is becoming a merciful person because he has received mercy. He pursues intimacy with God that results in personal holiness so that he might see the Lord in all things. His consuming passion is to help others find peace with God and one another. And though he will experience persecution because of his revolutionary commitment to Christ, he will endure all these things and grow for the gospel's sake.

In the words of Paul, the godly leader says,

> What is more, I consider everything a loss compared to the surpassing greatness of knowing Christ Jesus my Lord, for whose sake I have lost all things. I consider them rubbish, that I may gain Christ and be found in him, not having a righteousness of my own that comes from the law, but that which is through faith in Christ—the righteousness that comes from God and is by faith. I want to know Christ and the power of his resurrection and the fellowship of sharing in his sufferings, becoming like him in his death, and so, somehow, to attain to the resurrection from the dead. (Philippians 3:8-11)

As we lead the followers by following the Leader, others will want to join the ranks. This is the Master's plan for leadership multiplication! We will recruit by our Christlike example as we hold high the standards found in Matthew 5. By our lives and by our teaching, we can say:

Blessed are the humble.

Blessed are the broken.

Blessed are the submissive.

Blessed are the dependent.

Blessed are the merciful.

Blessed are those who hunger and thirst for righteousness.

Blessed are the peacemakers.

Blessed are the persecuted.

Blessed are those who are the salt of the earth and the light of the world.

Is there hope for the church whose leaders embrace our Lord's emphasis on godly character in Matthew 5?

Yes, indeed!

✍ LEADERSHIP REFLECTIONS

1. Reflect on your own "character." What kind of "characters" are a part of your leadership team? Do they match Jesus' perspective?
2. How can you implement Jesus' standard in your and your church's leadership?

ENDNOTES

Introduction—A Church in Search of Leadership

1. George Barna, *The Frog in the Kettle* (Ventura, CA: Regal Books, 1990), p. 138.
2. Ibid.
3. Ibid., pp. 137-138.
4. Ibid., p. 138.
5. Ibid., p. 137.
6. Ibid., pp. 135, 137.
7. Statistics supplied by Jean Fuchs, Office of Records and Research, The Christian and Missionary Alliance, Colorado Springs, CO, 1989.
8. Ibid.
9. Cited by Mary Francis Preston, *Christian Leadership* (Nashville: Convention Press, 1934), p. 19.
10. LeRoy Eims, *Be the Leader You Were Meant to Be* (Wheaton, IL: Scripture Press, 1975), p. 7.
11. Peter Wagner, *Leading Your Church to Growth* (Ventura, CA: Gospel Light, 1984), p. 73.

Chapter 1—The Wealth of a Poor Spirit

1. David Johnson with Tom Allen, *Joy Comes in the Mourning* (Camp Hill, PA: Christian Publications, 1998), pp. 11-12.
2. Gary L. Thomas, *The Glorious Pursuit* (Colorado Springs, CO: NavPress, 1998), p. 48.
3. Allan Bloom, *The Closing of the American Mind* (New York: Simon & Schuster, 1981), p. 173.
4. Johnson and Allen, p. 18.
5. A.W. Tozer, *The Knowledge of the Holy* (New York: Harper & Row, 1961), p. 13.
6. David E. Schroeder, *Follow Me: The Master's Plan for Men* (Camp Hill, PA: Christian Publications, 1993), p. 54.

Chapter 2—Joy in the Mourning

1. Johnson and Allen, p. 39.
2. Ibid., p. 51.

Chapter 3—The Strength of Submission

1. Johnson and Allen, p. 59.
2. John P. Kotter, "What Leaders Really Do," *Harvard Business Review* 3 (May-June, 1990), p. 107.
3. D. Martin Lloyd-Jones, *Studies in the Sermon on the Mount* (Grand Rapids, MI: Eerdmans, 1959), p. 281.

Chapter 4—In Dependence

1. Johnson and Allen, pp. 95-96.
2. Ibid., pp. 108-109.
3. A. W. Tozer, *The Pursuit of God* (Camp Hill, PA: Christian Publications, 1958), pp. 21-22.

Chapter 5—Merciful Heavens!

1. William Shakespeare, *The Merchant of Venice*, Act IV.
2. Charles Colson, "Making the World Safe for Religion," *Christianity Today*, November 8, 1993, p. 33.
3. D. Martyn Lloyd-Jones, *Studies in the Sermon on the Mount* (Grand Rapids, MI: Eerdmans, 1959), pp. 96-97.
4. Johnson and Allen, p. 117.

Chapter 6—Wholly Holy

1. Johnson and Allen, p. 142.
2. George Barna, *The Power of Vision* (Ventura, CA: Regal Books, 1992), p. 28.
3. Colin Brown, Editor, *New International Dictionary of New Testament Theology*, s.v. "Heart" by Theo Sorg, Volume 2, p. 182.

Chapter 7—The Peacemakers

1. William Hendriksen, *Exposition of the Gospel According to Matthew*, Vol. 1 of New Testament Commentary (Grand Rapids, MI: Baker Book House, 1973), p. 278.

2. Jerry Bridges, *The Practice of Godliness* (Colorado Springs, CO: NavPress, 1983), p. 194.

3. Richard F. Lovelace, *Dynamics of Spiritual Life* (Downers Grove, IL: InterVarsity Press, 1979), pp. 204-208.

4. Johnson and Allen, p. 176.

Chapter 8—Testing One, Two, Three

1. Johnson and Allen, p. 194.

2. Ibid., p. 201.

3. William Barclay, *The Gospel of Matthew* (Philadelphia, PA: Westminster, 1958), p. 108.

4. Ibid., p. 106.

5. Ibid., p. 108.

6. Ibid.

Chapter 9—Oh, to Be Like Him!

1. Thomas O. Chisholm, "Oh, to Be Like Thee, Blessed Redeemer," *Hymns of the Christian Life* (Camp Hill, PA: Christian Publications, 1978), p. 231.

2. Arthur T. Pierson, *The Acts of the Holy Spirit* (Camp Hill, PA: Christian Publications, 1980), p. 22.

3. Ibid., p. 23.

LEADING *the* FOLLOWERS *by* FOLLOWING *the* LEADER

STUDY AND APPLICATION GUIDE

Kit Kindred
and Dennis L. Gorton

Introduction

The purpose of this guide is to put you in situations where you will be stretched and have the opportunity to develop Christlike character. It is out of interpersonal relationships, conflict resolution and prayerful self-examination that character can grow and develop. Much of the group application will demand an openness that might make you feel vulnerable. Yet by risking vulnerability we have the opportunity to walk humbly in our relationships with others. Such practice soon develops character.

See the study as a journey of growth. Each chapter will have study questions reflecting on your knowledge of the reading. It will have a personal application focused on honest self-examination before the Lord. Finally, it will have a group application that will involve you in developing closer interpersonal relationships with the other leaders. Together you have the opportunity to encourage and hold each other accountable. Remember that character is far more important than position. Expect God to interact with you as He challenges you through these chapters.

CHAPTER 1

Study: The Wealth of a Poor Spirit

1. How does Chapter 1 compare Jesus' ministry to what might seem poor church growth strategy?

_____

_____

_____

2. What did you read that would suggest humility must be the priority of leaders?

_____

_____

_____

3. Why did the Pharisees make poor leaders?

_____

_____

_____

4. From your reading of the chapter, how would you say humility is displayed?

_____

_____

_____

5. What challenges you most from this chapter?

_____

_____

_____

Personal Application

Spend some time in prayer, worshiping God and asking Him to show you any areas of pride in your life.

1. Focus on God's Character:
   - Psalm 46:10-11
   - Psalm 145:8-9
   - Isaiah 6:1-3, 5
   - Jeremiah 9:23-24
   - Philippians 2:5-8
   - Romans 5:8-10
2. Confession of Sin
   Consider and check the following:
   - ☐ People I am serving do not know I love them
   - ☐ My leadership style hurts others
   - ☐ My prayer life tells God I am self-sufficient
   - ☐ I am bitter because of past conflicts
   - ☐ I am more like the Pharisees in leadership than Jesus
   - ☐ I expect recognition from others
   - ☐ I have forgotten I am a sinner saved by grace
   - ☐ I do not walk in humble dependence on God

My Prayer of Confession

Heavenly Father, I recognize my sinful pride and now confess and repent for _____

_____

_____

Make me what you want me to be. Make me a humble servant.

In Jesus' name, Amen.

Group Application: Humility and Accountability

Many Christians find it hard to admit their struggles to each other. *What will he think of me? What will he say? Will he tell someone what I told him in privacy?* Yet James 5:16 calls us to confess our sins to one another. It is very humbling to admit our struggles and pray for each other. It demands confidentiality, humility and mercy.

1. Go around the room and share a time when confessing your struggle to a friend was helpful and encouraging.
2. In groups of two or three share a personal struggle and pray for each other.

CHAPTER 2

Study: Joy in the Mourning

1. Based on your reading of Chapter 2, why is repentance so important for us?

   _____

   _____

   _____

2. What does this chapter tell us about brokenness? How is it displayed?

   _____

   _____

   _____

3. Reconciliation pictures two enemies working through their differences to the point of becoming friends. List the steps that would have to be taken for two people to be reconciled.

   _____

   _____

   _____

4. God puts a high value on relationships. What could you do that would better express the high value God wants us to place on relationships?

_____

_____

_____

5. What challenges you the most from this chapter?

_____

_____

_____

Personal Application

1. Check one in each set of three that best describes how you act in a conflict. Be honest before God.

A. ☐ 1. I avoid expressing my opinion.
    ☐ 2. I try to ask good questions to understand others.
    ☐ 3. I use logical arguments to persuade others.

B. ☐ 1. I use silence in disputes.
    ☐ 2. I use a stern tone in conflict.
    ☐ 3. I work at being calm and compassionate.

C. ☐ 1. I am quick to speak and slow to listen.
    ☐ 2. I am a good listener in conflict.
    ☐ 3. I tend to avoid those I'm in conflict with.

D. ☐ 1. I get in people's faces.
    ☐ 2. I persevere through conflict with others.
    ☐ 3. I withdraw from arguments.

E. ☐ 1. I speak honestly, but gently
    ☐ 2. I passively listen to lectures
    ☐ 3. I lecture others

F. ☐ 1. I feel defeated in most disputes.
    ☐ 2. I see conflict as a chance to grow.
    ☐ 3. I get angry easily.

G. ☐ 1. My goal is to convince others of the right
           way.
    ☐ 2. My goal is resolution and reconciliation.
    ☐ 3. My goal is peace at any cost.

H. ☐ 1. No one ever doubts my opinion.
    ☐ 2. I am equally concerned that all views are
           considered.
    ☐ 3. I seldom express my opinion.

I. ☐ 1. I say I am sorry often in conflicts.
    ☐ 2. I work at repenting when I'm in the wrong.
    ☐ 3. I explain why it is others' fault as much as
           mine.

J. ☐ 1. I get strong in my expressions.
    ☐ 2. I see others as teammates rather than oppo-
           nents.
    ☐ 3. I tell others only part of my opinion.

2. *Evaluation of conflict style:* Place a check mark next
   to the number of the statement you marked in
   sections A-J of the previous questionnaire and total the number of check marks to get your score.

	PASSIVE/ AVOIDERS		AGGRESSIVE/ CONTENDERS		LOVING/ COMMUNI-CATORS
A1		A3		A2	
B1		B2		B3	
C3		C1		C2	
D3		D1		D2	
E2		E3		E1	
F1		F3		F2	
G3		G1		G2	
H3		H1		H2	
I1		I3		I2	
J3		J1		J2	
TOTAL					

3. My style is most often_____
4. What specific area of conflict could you repent of?
   I will stop_____
   I will start_____
5. Prayer

   Heavenly Father, I am sorry and want to repent of
   _____. *Help me to start*

   _____
   _____ *in my disputes*
   with others. I sincerely desire to change.
   In Jesus' name, Amen.

Group Application

It is a prideful and ugly event when God's leaders mistreat each other. God has given us clear instructions on how to treat each other in disputes. Yet all too often Christian leaders revert to childish responses in the midst of conflict. The Corinthians were infamous in this regard. Paul rebuked them in First Corinthians 6:5-8:

> I say this to shame you. Is it possible that there is nobody among you wise enough to judge a dispute between believers? But instead, one brother goes to law against another—and this in front of unbelievers!
>
> The very fact that you have lawsuits among you means you have been completely defeated already. Why not rather be wronged? Why not rather be cheated? Instead, you yourselves cheat and do wrong, and you do this to your brothers.

Humility guards the other person's dignity. Humility would rather be wronged. Humility considers the other person first. "Do nothing out of selfish ambition or vain conceit, but in humility consider others better than yourselves" (Philippians 2:3). It is time to be held accountable.

Assignment

Check the following areas of sin that turn disagreements into ugly clashes. I struggle with:

☐ angry, aggressive outbursts
☐ passively withdrawing to protect myself

- ☐ being quick to speak and slow to listen
- ☐ gossip and backbiting
- ☐ condemning attitudes toward others
- ☐ not giving gentle answers
- ☐ the need to be right
- ☐ intolerance of others' opinions
- ☐ wanting to make everyone happy
- ☐ spiritual pride that I have the answers
- ☐ seeing myself better than others
- ☐ using intimidation tactics
- ☐ not praying for God's answer for the conflict

_____ is someone I have an unresolved conflict with; I need to go to him or her and begin a process of reconciliation, which includes:

- Humbly confessing our sinful tendencies to each other.
- Praying regularly for each other.
- Holding each other accountable for our response to disputes.

Remember that learning to walk humbly before God and others is a process that takes time and effort. If you need a mediator to resolve a dispute, seek the advice of this group of leaders.

CHAPTER 3

Study: The Strength of Submission

1. After reading about the characteristic of meekness, define and describe it in your own words.

_____

_____

_____

2. Why isn't meekness considered by many as a leadership quality?

_____

_____

_____

3. Why is meekness so important to God?

_____

_____

_____

4. Based on your reading, how is meekness (submission to God) displayed in relationships?

_____

_____

_____

5. What challenges you most from this chapter?

_____

_____

_____

Personal Application

"Wow—can you believe what just happened here in our church?" Two weeks before a special guest had been invited to speak. The speaker had agreed to share for ten minutes about his ministry and solicit prayer for it. Unfortunately, the speaker had taken liberties, speaking for almost half an hour. In addition, he had said and done some things that many people felt were out of line with Scripture. As a result, a number of people were confused and asking serious questions.

So on this Sunday, one of the elders stood and admitted that he and the other leaders had failed the congregation by not speaking to the improprieties in the service. The pastor stood after the elder's apology and admitted that he had been so concerned about preaching his sermon that he had failed in his pastoral duty by not immediately addressing the things that occurred in the service. He, too, asked for forgiveness.

1. Heart Check
Before God, honestly answer the following questions:

- How would I respond to the elders and pastor admitting their mistake and asking for forgiveness?

- Do I trust God to use my pastor and elders to guide, teach and correct me?
- Did the leaders demonstrate meekness, humility and submission? How? Be specific.

2. The Humble Conversation

The kingdom of God is reserved for servant leaders. None of us deserves that place. All too often church leaders cling to positions as if they own them. They fight for control of the church. God is looking for servants to lead. Servants give up their rights. Servants surrender control to their master. Servants see themselves as unworthy. Therefore, God gives them grace to lead in love.

Group Application

1. In His Presence

Spend half of your group time in prayers of worship and adoration. Focus on God's attributes and character. Come to God in submission and brokenness.

Begin with these Scriptures:
- Isaiah 6:1-5
- Jeremiah 9:23-24
- Exodus 33:7-18 and 34:5-8

2. After this time of worship and prayer, discuss the following questions.
   - What attribute or characteristic of God is most meaningful to you in this time of your life?
   - What is God teaching you in the process of submitting yourself and your ministry to your Lord and to each other as leaders?

- Who are our "enemies" (the difficult ones) in our church and how do we demonstrate God's love to them?

Assignment

As a leader in your church, set up a time with the pastor to discuss:

a. Specific ways that leaders can model a spirit of meek leadership to the congregation.

b. Actions that leaders can take to be servants to their people.

c. Specific ways that leaders can turn the other cheek, go the second mile, give away their coat and shirt.

CHAPTER 4

Study:
In Dependence

1. In your own words, what does it mean to be hungry for something?

   _____

   _____

   _____

2. According to the chapter, how is a hunger for righteousness displayed?

   _____

   _____

   _____

3. Describe the problem of pseudo-holiness.

   _____

   _____

   _____

4. How is Christ's standard of righteousness attainable?

   _____

   _____

   _____

5. What challenges you most from this chapter?

_____

_____

_____

Personal Application

How we spend our time and money tells a lot about us. In this personal application, evaluate one week of your life by answering the following questions for each segment of the weekly chart on the next page.

Questions:

1. Was God part of this segment of my week?

_____

2. If so, how? _____

_____

_____

3. If not, how could I make Him part of this segment? _____

_____

_____

SUN	MON	TUES	WED	THURS	FRI	SAT
MORNING	MORNING	MORNING	MORNING	MORNING	MORNING	MORNING
AFTERNOON	AFTERNOON	AFTERNOON	AFTERNOON	AFTERNOON	AFTERNOON	AFTERNOON
EVENING	EVENING	EVENING	EVENING	EVENING	EVENING	EVENING

Group Application

1. Go around the circle of leaders and answer the following two questions:
   - What will it take for me to live in constant dependence on God?
   - What will it cost me to do so?
2. Go around the circle and pray for the one to your right.

CHAPTER 5

Study:
Merciful Heavens!

1. Define mercy in your own words.

_____

_____

_____

2. How is mercy Christlike?

_____

_____

_____

3. Why is mercy a risky business?

_____

_____

_____

4. What hinders us from being merciful?

_____

_____

_____

5. What challenges you most from this chapter?

_____

_____

_____

Personal Application

She was caught in adultery. Everyone had a stone, ready for their brutal form of justice. She was scared, embarrassed and all alone in this circle of judges. Tears rolled down her cheeks as she cringed before them. She would die for her sins.

A hush grew over the crowd as a Man stepped into the circle. He wrote words in the dirt that made their hearts cringe. He looked them in the eye. They turned away. An uneasy feeling flooded the air. "He who is without sin can cast the first stone." In the next minute there was no one left. The woman now stared at this Man in disbelief. She would not be dying for her sins—He would.

It is when we see ourselves as not needing His mercy that we have no mercy. It is when we cannot see ourselves in her place that we justify ourselves and stand in judgment of others.

1. Who have you withheld mercy from?

_____

_____

_____

2. As God brings the names of any persons to mind, repent for your spiritual pride and beg Jesus' forgiveness.

_____

_____

_____

3. If you feel that you need to apologize to anyone for having a judgmental attitude toward him, ask God to give you the strength to do it and to show you the words to say.

_____

_____

_____

Group Application

Discuss the following questions:

1. How can we display a desire for holiness yet show mercy to those in sin?
2. How can we demonstrate more love and compassion for the lost around us? (neighbors, friends, relatives and coworkers)
3. What risks might I have to take in showing such love?

CHAPTER 6

Study:
Wholly Holy

1. After reading the text, what would you say it means to be pure in heart?

   _____

   _____

   _____

2. Describe the issue of impurity in the lives of the Pharisees. What did Jesus say about them?

   _____

   _____

   _____

3. How can we keep the issue of holiness focused on inner purity rather than outward conformity?

   _____

   _____

   _____

4. What is the connection between inward and outward purity?

   _____

   _____

   _____

5. What challenges you most from this chapter?

_____

_____

_____

Personal Application

Describe your pursuit of God in a paragraph. How have you sought to know Him? Describe how your relationship has grown. Before you write it, you may want to look at David's pursuit of God as found in Psalm 63.

_____

_____

_____

_____

_____

_____

_____

_____

Group Application

As a group, brainstorm how you could be more passionate about your love for God. After you make a list of ideas, evaluate which ones would be the best to apply to your lives. Then take time to discuss how you could put one or two into practice. Character is changed in the midst of relationships. As we work at our relationship with Jesus, certainly the character of purity will be evidenced in our lives.

LEADERSHIP PRINCIPLE 7: PEACEMAKING

CHAPTER 7

Study:
The Peacemakers

1. What does this chapter tell us abut peace in our relationship with God?

_____

_____

_____

2. Describe in what ways we can be peacemakers.

_____

_____

_____

3. How does a vital relationship with God enable us to influence others for Christ?

_____

_____

_____

4. According to the chapter, what is essential in making a good peacemaker?

_____

_____

_____

5. What challenges you most from this chapter?

_____

_____

_____

Personal Application

This chapter discusses peacemaking from both a vertical perspective (bringing people to God) and a horizontal perspective (bringing people into proper relationship with one another).

1. What are you doing this week to help bring people into relationship with Christ?

_____

_____

_____

2. What are you doing to motivate others to share their faith?

_____

_____

_____

3. Examine your heart to see if you have a "clear conscience" before your brothers in the Lord.

_____

_____

_____

Take a moment to surrender these issues to God. Believe He will handle them better than you ever could.

Group Application

Peacemaking always has the goal of reconcilia-tion. To be reconciled means that a new and better relationship has resulted through the efforts of two enemies working diligently through the peacemak-ing process. That does not mean we have to have a perfect relationship with all people but we can agree to disagree and seek to love one another.

The illegitimate process is when someone says they are sorry, the other says, "I forgive you" and they shake hands—but afterwards are distant at best. Too often we have shortchanged the peacemaking pro-cess.

Consider the following pattern of God's example of peacemaking. Discuss how we can follow His ex-ample:

- 1 John 4:19   He sought us first.

- Isaiah 1:18   He confronts and seeks col-laboration.

- 1 John 2:2   Restitution was made.

- Acts 17:30-31   God asks us to take responsi-bility and do the right thing.
  Mark 1:15   (Repent.)

- 1 John 1:9   As we repent, God responds by forgiving us and restoring the relationship.

- 2 Corinthians 5:17-20   We are called to be in healthy relationship so we can act as reconcilers between God and man.

CHAPTER 8

Study: Testing One, Two, Three

1. What are the reasons Christians face persecution?

_____

_____

_____

2. In your own words explain external and internal persecution.

_____

_____

_____

3. What can we do to stay strong during such persecution?

_____

_____

_____

4. How can we avoid becoming party to internal persecution?

_____

_____

_____

5. What challenges you most from this chapter?

_____

_____

_____

Personal Application

1. What thoughts and reactions do you tend to have when facing opposition or persecution?

_____

_____

_____

2. God continually brings us back to the same lessons until we submit to his teaching. A friend of mine worked hard at making everyone around him happy. He wanted peace at any cost. This forced him to change churches a number of times. God impressed Galatians 1:10 on his heart years before he did much about it: "Am I now trying to win the approval of men, or of God? Or am I trying to please men? If I were still trying to please men, I would not be a servant of Christ."

   He knew he should stop being such a people pleaser, but in reality he wanted men's approval more than God's approval. It made him miserable. Finally, he realized there was no escaping the issue. He was in a church of many legalists. These legalists were more concerned with outward conformity than an inward relationship of holy love for God.

   My friend was very gifted at bringing people to Jesus. The problem was many church folks were very critical of these new believers. He was torn between his love for his new converts and his fear of what the legalists of his church might think of him. He called me and we sat down and considered what Jesus would want him to do.

Group Application

It takes a deep level of commitment to Christ and each other to address the underlining issues that cause internal persecution in the church. Yet if we are to ever have healthy churches and develop the quality of personal perseverance, we must be willing to be honest about it. As a guide for discussion, answer the following questions.

1. Do we display legalistic rules in our church that hinder people from finding a real and meaningful love relationship with Jesus?
2. Do we allow sinful practices to continue in our church because we are afraid of dealing with them?
3. Are there traditions in this church that are more important than the biblical mandate to be a Great Commission church?
4. Are we as leaders more concerned about keeping the peace at any cost than loyally serving Christ no matter what the cost?

After the discussion, spend some time in prayer and then set a plan of action in response to what God is asking you to do.

Assignment

Open the Scriptures and write out a plan that would help my friend face this persecution and yet do the right thing.

CHAPTER 9

Study: Oh, to Be Like Him!

1. According to our study, what is the main purpose of salt? How does that describe our place as Christians?

_____

_____

_____

2. What part does the Holy Spirit play in accomplishing this?

_____

_____

_____

3. What does this chapter have to say about our purpose in our world?

_____

_____

_____

4. What does it mean to become tasteless salt? What can we do to remain salty?

_____

_____

_____

5. What challenges you most from this chapter?

_____

_____

_____

Personal Application

George slumped in his chair as we talked. I had been telling our elders how they could plant God's Word in the lives of others.

"All we have to do is share the things God is teaching us," I said. "Treat this subject like any other. The other day, my friend, Ted, was very frustrated with his partner at work. I told him of similar frustrations in my own life and what God had been teaching me about peacemaking."

"It's easy for you to talk with people," George told me. "You have things that are happening in your life. God is always teaching you something."

George had revealed something about his walk with God. He seldom had anything to share, because he seldom had anything new taking place in his walk with God. Being a witness demands a close walk with Jesus. It means I must treat Jesus as my companion—and more than a companion, as a friend and mentor, my master and guide. It is out of a living, daily relationship with Jesus that sowing the seed becomes natural and inspiring. That night George and I prayed for his walk with Jesus to be like that.

1. What has to change in your life for you to work closely with God?

   _____

   _____

   _____

2. Begin to pray for three lost friends that you can start to share with. Write their names below.

   _____

   _____

   _____

Group Application

1. Go around the room and share your biggest hindrance to being a witness for Christ. Examine issues such as self-centeredness, greed, pride, a poor relationship with Jesus, conflict with others, abrasiveness, defensiveness, bitterness, lust, apathy, etc.
2. Spend time in prayer and confession. Repent and ask God to change you—and believe that He will.

Study: New Hope for the Church

1. Write a paragraph contrasting a church that focuses on formulas versus a church that is built on character.

   _____

   _____

   _____

   _____

   _____

2. Describe what a leader will look like who is produced according to Matthew 5:3-10.

   _____

   _____

   _____

3. What is the most significant lesson you have learned from these studies?

   _____

   _____

   _____

Personal Application

1. Review your answer to question 5 of each study. List two or three of these and write a paragraph about how these impact your life.

_____

_____

_____

_____

_____

_____

_____

2. Review the personal application of each chapter. What application is most crucial for you to continue working on? What will you do to incorporate it into your lifestyle?

_____

_____

_____

Group Application

1. Discuss how you can encourage and hold each other accountable in your development of character.
2. What are the potential roadblocks to continuing this process?
3. What can you do to overcome these roadblocks?
4. Spend time in prayer asking God to knit you together as you work on these character issues.

SELECTED BIBLIOGRAPHY

Barclay, William. *The Gospel of Matthew*. Philadelphia: Westminster Press, 1958.

Barna, George. *The Frog in the Kettle*. Ventura, CA: Regal Books, 1990.

————. *The Power of Vision*. Ventura, CA: Regal Books, 1992.

Bird, Charles. *Social Psychology*. New York: Appleton-Century, 1940.

Blake, Robert R. and Mouton, J.S. *The Managerial Grid*. Houston: Gulf Publishing Company, 1964.

————. *The New Managerial Grid*. Houston: Gulf Publishing Company, 1964.

Bloom, Allan. *The Closing of the American Mind*. New York: Simon and Schuster, 1981.

Bridges, Jerry. *The Practice of Godliness*. Colorado Springs: NavPress, 1983.

Centennial Advance Achievements. Nyack, NY: Christian and Missionary Alliance, 1987.

Coleman, Robert. *The Master Plan of Evangelism*. Old Tappan, NJ: Fleming H. Revell, 1963.

Division of Church Ministries, *Churches Planting Churches*. Nyack, NY: The Christian and Missionary Alliance, 1987.

Dobbins, Gaines S. *Learning to Lead*. Nashville: Broadman Press, 1968.

Eims, LeRoy. *Be the Leader You Were Meant to Be*. Wheaton, IL: Scripture Press, 1975.

Engstrom, Ted W. *The Making of a Christian Leader*. Grand Rapids: Zondervan, 1978.

George, Norman and von Der Embge, T.J. "Six Proportions for Managerial Leadership: Diagnostic Tools for Definition and Focus." *Business Horizons*, December, 1971.

Greenleaf, Robert K. *Servant Leadership*. New York: Paulist Press, 1977.

Hendrikson, William. *Exposition of the Gospel According to Matthew*. Vol. 2 of New Testament Commentary. Grand Rapids: Baker Book House, 1973.

Hunter, George G., ed. *The Bridges of Contagious Evangelism: Social Networks in Church Growth, State of the Art*. Wheaton, IL: Tyndale House Publishers, 1986.

Johnson, David and Allen, Tom. *Joy Comes in the Mourning*. Camp Hill, PA: Christian Publications, 1998.

Kotter, John P. "What Leaders Really Do." *Harvard Business Review*, May-June, 1990.

Likert, Rensis. *New Patterns of Management*. New York: McGraw-Hill, 1961.

Lloyd-Jones, D. Martyn. *Studies in the Sermon on the Mount*. Grand Rapids: Eerdmans, 1959.

Lovelace, Richard F. *Dynamics of Spiritual Life*. Downers Grove, IL: InterVarsity Press, 1979.

Mavis, W. Curry. *Advancing the Smaller Church*. Winona Lake, IN: Light and Life Press, 1957.

McGavran, Donald. *Modern Church Growth*. Grand Rapids: Eerdmans, 1982.

McMillen, S.I. *None of These Diseases*. Westwood, NJ: Fleming H. Revell, 1963.

Mid-Centennial Review. Unpublished Report. Nyack, NY: Christian and Missionary Alliance, 1982.

New International Dictionary of New Testament Theology. Ed. C. Brown. s.v. "Kardia" by T. Sorg.

Perry, Lloyd. *Getting the Church on Target*. Chicago: Moody Press, 1981.

Peters, Tom. *A Passion for Excellence*. New York: Random House, 1985.

Pierson, A.T. *The Acts of the Holy Spirit*. Camp Hill, PA: Christian Publications, 1980.

Preston, Mary Francis. *Christian Leadership*. Nashville: Covington Press, 1934.

Schaller, Lyle B. *Activating the Passive Church*. Nashville: Abingdon Press, 1981.

Schaller, L.B. and Tidwell, Charles A. *Effective Church Planning*. Nashville: Abingdon Press, 1979.

Schroeder, David E. *Follow Me: The Master's Plan for Men*. Camp Hill, PA: Christian Publications, 1993.

Shawchuck, Norman. *Taking a Look at Your Leadership Styles*. Downers Grove, IL: Organizational Resources Press, 1980.

Stogdill, Ralph M. "Historical Trends in Leadership Theory and Research." *Journal of Contemporary Business*, Fall, 1974.

The Unchurched American—Ten Years Later. Princeton, NJ: Princeton Religious Research Center, 1988.

Tozer, A.W. *The Knowledge of the Holy*. New York: Harper & Rox, Publishers, Inc., 1961

———. *The Root of the Righteous*. Camp Hill, PA: Christian Publications, 1955.

Vicedom, George F. *A Prayer for the World*. St. Louis: Concordia, 1967.

Wagner, C. Peter. *Your Church Can Grow*. Ventura, CA: Regal Books, 1976.

———. *Leading Your Church to Growth*. Ventura, CA: Gospel Light Publishers, 1984.

———, ed. *Church Growth State of the Art*. Wheaton, IL: Tyndale House Publishers, 1986.